THE FAMILY AND EDUCATION

John Olsen, CFX and Thomas Masters (ed.)

THE FAMILY AND EDUCATION

To Teach As Jesus Did

New City Press

Published in the United States by New City Press
206 Skillman Avenue, Brooklyn, New York, 11211
© 1989 New City Press, New York

Cover photo by Meinolf Otto
Cover design by Nick Cianfarani

Library of Congress Cataloging-in-Publication Data:

The Family and Education : teaching as Jesus did / John Olsen and
Thomas Masters (ed.).
   p.   cm.
  ISBN 0-911782-73-7 : $6.95
  1. Family--Religious life.   2. Christian education--Home training.
3. Catholic Church--Education.   4. Spiritual life--Catholic authors.
I. Olsen, John, CFX.   II. Masters, Thomas.
BX2351.F3528   1989
248.8'45--dc20

                                    89-35976

Printed in the United States of America

CONTENTS

INTRODUCTION

The primary role of the family in Christian education as an essential element in the process of education has come to full awareness in our time. It is articulated in the writings of the Holy Father, Pope John Paul II, in the pastoral letters of the bishops and in the works of Catholic educators. It is experienced in the lives of parents and teachers in the schools and parishes, as well as in the home.

This awareness is not completely new. Pope Paul VI wrote in previous times that it is in the Christian family that the gospel is transmitted and radiated. Within the family, he said, "all the members evangelize and are evangelized" (Apostolic Exhortation, Evangelii Nuntiandi, *71:AAS 68 [1976] 60-61).*

Vatican II, in its "Declaration on Christian Education" has also stated this very clearly. We read there: "Since parents have conferred life on their children, they have a most solemn obligation to educate their offspring. . . . For, it devolves on parents to create a family atmosphere so animated with love and reverence for God and men that a well-rounded personal and social development is fostered among the children." (These phrases were first set forth by Pius XI in 1937, in the encyclical letter Divini Iluis Magestri.*)*

Most recently, Pope John Paul II wrote in his Apostolic Exhortation, The Role of the Christian Family in the Modern World, *"By virtue of their ministry of educating, parents are, through the witness of their lives, the first heralds of the gospel for their children."*

This emphasis of Pope John Paul II on the witness of the lived Christianity in the family is the essential charac-

teristic of this book. The reader will find here not only sound principles and exhortation but also the concrete experiences of living in the family in a Christian way, one informed by Christian values and beliefs.

The bishops of the United States gave specificity and clarity to this way of teaching and learning in the Christian family in their pastoral letter on Catholic education issued in November 1972, entitled To Teach as Jesus Did (TTJD). Here they presented three essential elements of Christian Education: MESSAGE, COMMUNITY, AND SERVICE. They stated clearly in this work the role of the family in the process. We read, for instance: "In the family children learn to believe what their parents' words and example teach about God, and parents enrich their own faith by participating in the formal religious education of their children." And, "Creating readiness for growth in community through worship and the events of everyday life is an integral part of the task of Catholic education, which also seeks to build community within its own programs and institutions." They added, "The experience of Christian community leads naturally to service. Christ gives his people different gifts not only for themselves but for others. Each must serve the other for the good of all." Here, then, we find the pedagogy for family education.

The family unity which nurtures that love and mutual charity which is at the heart of this center for Christian education has been a particular aspect of the spirituality of the Focolare Movement, a contemporary lay movement within the Church. This title, "Focolare," means fireplace or hearth. It is a symbol of the home, of the warmth and fire which sustains and energizes the relationship of the members of the family. The name was given to Chiara Lubich, the foundress, and to her early companions by those who witnessed the effects of mutual love and the

8

sustained effort to live out that phrase of the gospel, "Where two or three are gathered in my name, there I am in their midst" (Mt 18:20).

It is not surprising that Chiara has focused attention on the needs of the family today and through various meetings has shared wisdom and experience on ways in which families can become the centers for Christian education. One such meeting took as its theme "The Family and Education" and the talk of Chiara at the opening of this meeting is published here in its entirety. This talk provides the foundation out of which the practical and lived experiences of ordinary families who are seeking to be centers of love and Christian formation find deeper meaning and inspiration.

The twenty-four experiences in this book present the impact of the gospel on family life. They are real, but not in the sense that we may have become accustomed to think of "reality"—as the bizarre or the sensational. They are not presented because they are well-told tales (although they communicate the energy and vitality of any gripping story), or because they contain the solution to every problem a family might face (although they contain events as mundane as cleaning up the children's room to as dramatic as facing terminal illness), or because they will compel a reader to a particular organization. They are an attempt by these families, in their own words, to share the light that has come into their lives, which makes every situation they face another opportunity to grow closer to one another, to their neighbors and to God.

Some parents do ask if it is possible to live this way in the world we live in today. Yes, it is possible, as the experiences following the message of Chiara Lubich will illustrate. It is the hope that all who read these experiences may find in them encouraging models of what it means *"to teach as Jesus did,"* and will build in their own family setting Christian educational centers which are nourished on the message of the gospel and of their lives, on community, and on service.

May the light and life of such families bring much hope into a society searching for a new way.

THE ONE AND ONLY TEACHER
by Chiara Lubich

Dear friends,

I would like to begin by greeting all of you, especially those who have come from the farthest corners of the world.

The congress arranged by the New Families Movement is beginning today. The theme of the congress is "The family and education." My brief talk is intended simply as an introduction to such an important theme.

This congress will examine the theme in-depth, from different points of view. I would like to lay the foundation for all that will be said. If this foundation is put into life, I believe that everything will acquire more value and true value.

Speaking of education, we naturally find ourselves before two subjects: the educator or teacher, who must teach, and the disciple or pupil who must be educated.

With regard to the teacher, there is a phrase from the gospel which makes us think and which can shed light on the education which should be imparted in the family.

The sentence is: "One among you is your teacher, the rest are learners" (Mt 23:8). Jesus recognizes one teacher alone, he himself. This does not mean that he denies the presence of authority. This must be interpreted, however, not as a dominion or power, but as a service. This is because in service, which is love, it is not only the human person who acts, but Christ himself in the human person. In this way, Christ continues to be the first Teacher.

First of all, he gives example. He himself incarnates his doctrine. He does not impose burdens before carrying them himself: "Woe to you" he says, "You lay impossible burdens on men but will not lift a finger to lighten them!" (Lk 11:46). Jesus puts into practice what he asks of others.

Looking at him, we can deduce that the first way to educate, and this applies to parents as well, is not so much instructing or correcting, but living, with total commitment, one's own life as a Christian. Parents themselves must put into practice what they ask of their children. Do they ask for sincerity, commitment, loyalty, obedience, charity towards others, chastity, patience and forgiveness? Children should find these qualities, first of all, in their parents. Children should always be able to find in their mothers and fathers indisputable models to which they can relate.

Another characteristic of the way Jesus educated involves intervening with concrete assistance as he did when he calmed the storm on the lake (cf. Lk 8:24).

On a natural level, parents do everything they possibly can for their children. They will be able to do even more; above all, they will be able to do everything better, if they elevate their natural love to include a supernatural love; that is, if they love with God's charity, with the charity of one who takes the initiative in loving, without expecting anything in return. This is a love which never leaves others indifferent.

Moreover, Jesus has confidence in the people he teaches, as we can conclude from his words to the adulteress: "Go," he says, "and don't sin any more" (cf. Jn 8:11). He believes that it is possible for this woman to begin a life that is morally correct.

The words of parents must always be words of encouragement. They must be words charged with hope, positive words which express all their confidence in the new beginning of their children.

Jesus leaves each person free and responsible to make his or her own decisions, as he did when he met the rich young man (cf. Mt 19:16). We must never impose our own ideas, but offer them as expressions of love. First and foremost, children are sons and daughters of God, not ours alone. They should not be treated, therefore, as our possessions, but as persons who have been entrusted to us.

Jesus does not hesitate to correct, with decision and force when necessary. He says to Peter, who wanted to prevent him from facing his passion: "Get out of my sight, you satan! You are not judging by God's standards but by man's!" (Mt 16:23).

Correction is also necessary. It is an integral part of education: "He who loves his son is diligent to discipline him" (Pr 13:24), as is written in the sacred book of Proverbs. As father and teacher, God's education of the Hebrews, whom he formed himself, involved instruction and correction.

Woe to us if we do not discipline! We shall be responsible for such an omission! This passage from the Prophet Ezekiel is particularly striking: "If you do not warn the wicked man to renounce his ways, then he shall die for his sin, but I will hold you responsible for his death" (Ezk 33:8). Correction is therefore the duty of parents. Admonishment, given with peace, calm and detachment, increases the sense of responsibility on the part of the children who will always remember it.

In the stupendous parable of the prodigal son, Jesus shows us the father's mercy and therefore, his mercy towards those who repent and return to what is good. Parents must treat their children as God treats us.

The mercy of a father and mother in a family must reach the point of truly knowing how to forget, how to "cover over everything" (1 Cor 13:7) with God's charity. Repeated reminders of a negative past are not in line with Jesus' way of thinking. This explains why they are not accepted.

Jesus teaches in the synagogue, on the mountain, along the roads of Galilee and Judea, in the temple of Jerusalem. Likewise, any place can be useful to parents for teaching.

Jesus' way of expressing himself is new, although he keeps to the customs of his time. He speaks a language that is alive, filled with images, concrete, brief and precise. He avoids any kind of long-windedness. He often condenses into one phrase all that he has to say on a particular subject.

This is what should be done in the family. The so-called long "sermons" are not accepted by our young people. A few words are enough, offered by a true, pure and selfless love. Jesus also uses dialogue, alternating questions and answers. He uses maxims, and, with the scribes and Pharisees, discussion.

The dialogue between parents and sons or daughters, whether they be children or adults, must never be interrupted. It must always be open, serene and constructive, as between friends.

In many families, there are sons or daughters who turn away, despite the witness given by their parents who have tried to live according to the gospel. At times, they also drift from the faith. The relationship with these sons and daughters must never be broken no matter which pathway they follow, even if they follow ideologies which are distant from God; even if they follow the pathway of drugs or of experiences which are radically in contrast with the moral teaching they had received in the family.

Particularly in the West, we are immersed in a secularized society in which important traditional values have faded away, and new ones emerged: there is a strong awareness of personal freedom for example, excitement over scientific and technological progress and the overcoming of cultural and national barriers, a different understanding of the role of women in today's society, and so on.

Parents must be able to discern. While communicating with their children, they must be mindful of the profound changes that have taken place in the context in which their children are living.

They need to know how to interpret the "signs of the times" which can be found in some of the new demands expressed by their children. While educating people, Jesus is not afraid to overturn the traditional scale of values, as when he announces the beatitudes (cf. Mt 5:2). He calls "happy," in fact, those who do not appear to be so. He presents a pathway which is difficult to take, and which is in opposition to what the world offers.

We too must have the courage to state what is truly of value. We must not deceive ourselves, thinking that by presenting a watered-down Christianity and a fictitious Christ, our proposals will be more readily accepted.

God makes himself heard in the hearts of our children. They react in a positive way only to the truth, when this is presented to them with a language that is accessible and acceptable; that is, when it is expressed by parents who, before teaching, have made the effort to understand and to share profoundly in the true demands of the new generations.

The gospel depicts Jesus speaking "as one who has authority" (Mt 7:29). Parents—trusting in the grace that they have as parents—must never neglect their responsibility as educators. Deep down in their hearts, children require this of them. It is for this very reason that children are often capable of judging their parents ruthlessly if they have been silent about the truth.

Jesus educates by passing on to his disciples "his" typical teaching: "This is my commandment: that you love one another, as I have loved you" (Jn 15:12). By specifying that "as I have loved you," Jesus presents himself as the "Master" of such love.

This must be the teaching, par excellence, which parents give to their children, because it is the synthesis of the gospel. Parents must imitate Jesus so well in putting it into practice, that they can repeat this commandment to their children as their own: my children, love one another as I have loved you.

Thus, we must imitate Jesus. We must imitate him as Teacher. We must imitate Jesus, or better still, we must allow him to live in us. Yes, by far, the best way would be if Jesus himself were to take our place. If he lives in us, our efforts as educators will be beyond reproach. If he becomes the educator in our families, we will carry out our responsibility perfectly.

Jesus must live in us, he must take our place. How can this come about? The gospel gives us the answer. We were still at the beginning of our new way of life when the Lord urged us to turn it into a divine adventure in which he would be present in us. Then, little by little, implanting in our minds the various ideas that gave rise to the spirituality of unity, the Spirit explained to us how this could become a reality.

Now all those who follow this pathway know how they should act so that Jesus may be in them. We must live the "new self," not the "old self." We must love in a supernatural way, being "outside of ourselves," as we say, always overcoming any obstacles that might turn up, by loving Jesus crucified and forsaken.

We should not live for ourselves. We must live for the others, "making ourselves one" with them in everything except sin. All these expressions tell us how Jesus can take his place within us. Jesus was already present in our soul through grace. Now he is more fully present because we correspond to this grace. Yes, by living in this way, Jesus is in us, Jesus the Teacher.

But Jesus must also live in the midst of our families. This is the presence of Jesus that comes about in unity, wherever two or more are united in his name (cf. Mt 18:20). Jesus between husband and wife; between mother and son; between father and daughter; between mother and grandfather or aunt. If Jesus is present among two or more members of our family, his influence as teacher and educator will be greater.

How can we guarantee this precious presence of his in our midst? We know the answer: by nourishing it every day, by rebuilding unity whenever it has been shattered, and by keeping ourselves open to one another, indeed, by going out of ourselves towards the other members of our family. I say, going out of ourselves towards the others, because in a family, the first neighbors to love are the members of one's own family. . . .

Precisely because we have put aside everything, at least spiritually, in order to follow Jesus ("If any man comes to me without hating his father, mother, wife, children, brothers, sisters, yes and his own life too, he cannot be my disciple"), we now hear him repeating to us these words: You do not love me if you do not love your family, first of all. Thus, whether we are alone or whether others in our family live the gospel, Jesus, the Teacher, will be present there.

The children who grow up in these families will be a new generation. Together with the life and nourishment they receive from their parents, and with all the affection and assistance that this first social cell offers, they will also be imbued with many of Jesus' ideas — Jesus' evangelical ideas.

Consequently, they will grow up reasoning as he reasons. They will learn to see humanity as the great family of God's children. They will no longer believe blindly in other systems; they will believe in the gospel. No relationship will attract them more than that based on Jesus' new commandment. These children will be new.

Thus the divine life received in baptism will be strengthened. Parents will put into action the graces that the sacrament of matrimony has placed at their disposal for the good of their children. Parents will collaborate with God in developing and rearing his children.

To educate, to transform the children and the entire family! To make of the family a small church, a dynamic reality open to the society around it and to its needs, orienting the children to look beyond themselves, to others and their needs!

It is a very lofty objective, and in certain cases, it may seem to be unattainable. But we should never despair. On the contrary, we should confidently orient ourselves towards its realization. To understand what we should do, let us look at how the Spirit urged the entire Focolare to act, to make all become one.

In our movement, we have welcomed persons of other religions and non-believers. We love these persons as we love ourselves. We joyfully accept the commitments that they spontaneously take as integral parts of our large family. We share with them all the spiritual and material patrimony. We are the Focolare because they too are present. Without their presence, we would lose our identity.

It must be like this in our families as well. Whoever is a little distant from this or from any other Christian ideal, whoever has other ideas or another faith, must be welcomed by us not only with human love, but with super-natural love.

We must treasure and appreciate whatever they give to the family, however small this may be. We must know how to highlight the good ideas they have. We should make them participate, as much as possible, in the spiritual and material riches of the family.

In short, we should do all we can to love this son or daughter or these sons and daughters, so that although they have not yet received the light of faith, they return this love in some way.

Moreover, to make the family a small cell of the Focolare or a small church, which is synonymous, means to imitate the family of Nazareth, that family which lived with Jesus in their midst in the most concrete and divine way.

In order to compose this masterpiece, the members of the family of Nazareth loved one another in a supernatural way, which means out of love for God and not for themselves. Mary, who was the true mother of Jesus and true wife of Joseph, loved both of them not for herself, but for God. Joseph did not love Mary for himself. He loved her for God, and he loved the child Jesus for God, even though he was his foster father.

Yes, we must love for God. Our love is truly purified of human attachments if our spirit is always turned towards Jesus forsaken.

My dear friends, I could continue to demonstrate how all the elements of our spirituality are very suitable for guiding the life of the family. But you know this. Yes, with our ideal, we can have the Teacher in our home.

Today, let us renew the proposal which makes his presence possible there. On this foundation, everything will be meaningful—all that is offered to you by science and by experiences in the pedagogical field will also acquire value.

May Our Lady give us many united families for the good of society and of the Church. Through these families we will have, besides all the rest, powerful means for spreading the kingdom of God in the world.

And by reaching out to other families and to all of humanity the family will become ever more beautiful, more united and more holy. And isn't this what God expects from us in an age which demands mature and holy lay people?

PART ONE:
THE EXAMPLE OF LIVING
ACCORDING TO THE GOSPEL

In the first place, as Chiara Lubich reminded us, Jesus has put into practice what he asked of others. He gives the example; he himself incarnates his doctrine.

The example of living according to the gospel is the first and most powerful way in which Christian education takes place in the family. Parents put into practice, as teachers, those values and qualities which they find in the gospels and which they want their children to develop.

This is the first of three interlocking dimensions: the message revealed by God which the Church proclaims. Doctrine is not merely matter for the intellect, but it is, according to Saint Paul, a way of life: "Let us profess the truth in love and grow to the full maturity of Christ the head" (Eph 4:15).

Speaking of this, the American bishops said: "Faith involves intellectual acceptance but also much more. Through faith men have a new vision of God, the world, and themselves. They must not only accept the Christian message but act on it, witnessing as individuals and a community to all that Jesus said and did" (TTJD #19).

The experiences which follow are, in most cases, ordinary events of everyday living in a family, described in the words of a parent. They are attempts to model the role of teacher in the family according to the example given in the gospel by Jesus himself.

TURNING INDIFFERENCE
INTO ACCEPTANCE

For a long time I had been struggling within myself over a situation with one of our boys. He is in his twenties and has no interest in school and no skills to get a regular job. As he worked on and off with different kinds of side jobs, I held a general impression that he was immature and irresponsible. Hoping it would force him into growing up, I had reached the point of wanting him to leave home. My disappointment and frustration worked its way to indifference.

I happened one day to attend a seminar on family and education and learned of an address given by Chiara Lubich to an international congress held on a similar topic. I was struck by the words, "There is only one who is Teacher among us, Jesus in our midst. If we live with him, he will educate our children and ourselves as well . . . Parents must also put into practice what they ask of their children." This gave me a chance to examine my own situation. I realized I was not loving my son, and recognized that I needed to have a lot more patience. In working to renew this relationship, I felt guided by the thought of giving without looking for anything in return.

For a few weeks things went along fine, and my attitude toward him was changing for the better. One morning, however, when I thought he had already left for work, I went into his room and found him still sleeping. All the feelings that I thought were gone resurfaced. Once again, I began to judge him, certain that he would never make any progress. I was soon filled with resentment and anger. At the same time, however, I could not block out the conviction that helped me before, "We have only one Teacher . . . " I stopped for a moment and prayed for God's help. It was another moment of conversion for me, and I understood this struggle of ours in a new way. The more I put my own feelings aside, the more I wanted to know how my son must have been feeling. I saw a person disappointed in himself, someone who was confused, fearful and depressed.

I began to look for ways to show my concern for him. The little things of our everyday life offered me many chances to do so. For instance, as I was about to leave the house one morning, he asked me to iron his shirt. I simply made an extra effort to take care of that for him before I left. When he came in very late from work, I would get up to fix him something to eat and to keep him company. Moments such as these were very important in rebuilding our rapport.

One afternoon I tried to express to him my interest and concern for his future. He became very defensive. I kept my peace this time and continued to try to reach him, but he still rejected my intrusion. After he left the house, I started thinking the whole situation all over again. I couldn't figure out any longer what was right and what was wrong. Though I had no solution, I knew that I could at least renew my love for him and continue being patient.

A few days passed by. One evening, as I was on my way to bed, I saw him sitting alone in his room. I was about to continue on to my own room, but I was reminded of a passage from scripture, "Come to me all you who are weary . . . for my yoke is easy and my burden light" (Mt 11:28-30). I went over and sat quietly on his bed. After a few moments I said, "You look very sad tonight." He immediately opened up to me and shared many of his worries. He told me he was sorry for the way he was behaving saying, "I didn't want to listen because what you were saying was the truth." With humility he described what he was going through and how he felt about himself. I listened to him, refraining from interrupting with any of my own ideas. When he finished, I felt I understood him better and could even make a few suggestions. What to do was becoming clearer for the both of us. Everything seemed filled with Jesus' presence; the Teacher was among us.

A year has now gone by. Although my son's career is still unsettled, his attitude about himself has improved. He is no longer depressed and has a positive approach to trying different things. His attempts to pursue various kinds of jobs have become an education in itself. I do continue to encourage, and he feels free to tell me about everything — his fears, his failures, and his ambitions. The bond of unity between us is very strong. Love worked the miracle of turning indifference into acceptance.

D. R.

A HARMONIOUS HOME

One of the things that most indicates the tenor of our family is the way the house looks. We have tried hard to teach our children that out of love for the others in the family, they should keep order and make their rooms look beautiful, but it hasn't always worked. There were times, when evening after evening, as I entered the house and tried to avoid stepping on the books and toys, my first words would be "How can you all stand such a mess like this?"

I gradually came to the realization that my attitude wasn't producing good results at all. Sure, I could round the kids together to shape up the house, which would provide at least a temporary state of order, but it would also create tension between us. Besides, everything would soon be messy again. I knew by now that "forced labor" wasn't going to help them learn anything.

There was an episode that helped me begin a conversion in my ways of handling the cleanliness of the house. One day, I found the back bedroom in danger of disappearing under the rubble. It was worth declaring a disaster area. I was about to explode. I remembered though, that I had to be the first to love concretely, not the first to expect the love of the others. My firmness, I understood, had to be an expression of love, not of irritation.

It was a Saturday, and I did have some free time. So I decided to peacefully sit in the middle of the room (it was hard to even find a space) and help until all was cleaned up. Four hours later, we were still picking through the rubble. Five trash bags later, we were almost finished. I never lost my peace and neither did the kids. Afterwards, we maintained this attitude toward the chores of the house, and have been getting better at it since.

Now as I walk up the stairs, I still pick up pieces of paper here and there. As I wait for dinner, I'll vacuum the rug. I'll do the dishes after dinner (if I can get to them before my wife does) to relieve her for a while. But I am trying to learn how to do these little things, not because I want to have a clean house, but because I want the others to have one. I ask the kids for their help, so that they can learn and share in all the aspects of our family life. And they have been learning. Now it more often happens that as I walk in the door in the evening they'll rush to me and say, "Go look at my room" or "I vacuumed the rug for you."

In this way, I have noticed that while we are learning to keep the home in greater harmony, we are also learning to grow as a family concerned for one another.

S. L.

VALUES

Harry: One of the ways by which I judge myself as a parent is how well I am able to instill and nurture good values in my children. This experience involves my youngest daughter, Anne, who at age sixteen rejected the values I tried to pass on to her. Anne left home just before her eighteenth birthday to live with a relative, who turned out to be her boyfriend. This was an incredible suffering for me. Everything I had worked, hoped, and dreamed about for Anne seemed to be going up in smoke. We didn't speak for five months. Our relationship was broken. When we did begin to communicate again, it was in a very superficial way. Rosemary and I did not want to get involved in her "new" life for fear she would think we approved of it. Besides, Anne was so negative and wrapped up in herself that even our telephone conversations were difficult.

In the Fall, we attended a congress on family life in Chicago. We were preparing to share how love was renewing our own family relationships, when suddenly it dawned on me that I couldn't do it. I would have been a hypocrite. I had been judging Anne and her boyfriend Mike, disguising it as parental disapproval. I realized then that I had to accept everyone. I couldn't pick and choose. Together with Rosemary I decided to make a new start.

Rosemary: The first thing that we thought of doing was to invite them over for dinner. We anticipated their nervousness and they reluctantly accepted. We tried especially to help Mike feel welcomed into our family. In that atmosphere of love and acceptance, Mike had the courage to share his difficult upbringing, and that helped us to know how to relate with him better.

Harry: We also started calling them more often. During one of our phone calls, Anne told me that she was pregnant. I hesitated a few seconds before responding, a few seconds that seemed like several minutes. In those moments I felt anger, shame, failure, worry, and concern for her future. I had to bite my tongue to not openly say things that simply would not have been of any help. Instead, I asked for God's help, because I knew my words would be so important to our relationship. Anne listened as I told her how happy I was that she was going to have the child, and what a wonderful gift of God it was. There was both surprise and joy in Anne's voice, as she was probably expecting a much different reaction. We had begun again.

Rosemary: So in the past six months, Harry and I have jumped at opportunities to build a relationship with Anne and Mike. We have found ourselves doing all kinds of things, like driving them to the doctor, and then to the hospital for the baby's birth (it was a girl). We took late night phone calls, picked up a prescription for the baby, and kept an eye out for sales in the newspapers for baby items. We even picked up a high chair off the curb and Harry fixed it up for the baby.

Anne and Mike have asked our advice on taxes and how to buy a car. We also noticed open and positive Anne had become. But most heartening to us, Anne recently wanted to know what to do to have the baby christened.

R. and H. M.

A BIG SURPRISE

January brought a big surprise for my husband and me — we found out that I was pregnant and that our fifth child would be due in September. At the time, we had talked seriously about enrolling as foster parents, so the news of my pregnancy changed our plans. But we were excited with this new development and trusted that this was God's plan for our family.

The next step, we felt, was to think of the best way to break the news to the children. One evening at dinner, we decided to make the announcement. As a result, we saw our happiness multiplied four-fold. The children seemed thrilled as they poured out their questions concerning the baby growing inside their mommy. After dinner, we all went to the living room to watch a film which we borrowed from a friend. The film showed amazing close-up photography of the fascinating details of fertilization and the development of the tiny human person being nourished by the mother. It was really a beautiful moment spent together that helped all of us to appreciate the work of God in creating a new human being and to appreciate also our unique gifts as man and woman. In this atmosphere of openness and love, we were able to answer their questions emphasizing above all God's love for each one of us. The children felt very special and proud to be expecting a new member of the family. Now it was their turn to share the news. It wasn't long before our neighbors and friends at school knew all about the baby.

One afternoon, however, when I was about eleven weeks along, I started to bleed. Nick immediately came home to take care of the household so that I could lie down and rest. We called the doctor. His advice was to continue to rest and to make an appointment to come in for an ultrasound the next morning. By this time the children were home from school. It was an unusual feeling for me to be lying in bed while they and Dad prepared supper. I prayed and made the choice to accept whatever God's plan might be. I tried to replace my worry with the effort to live each passing moment well, thinking only of how to love those around me. At dinner, Nick explained to the children the serious situation we were facing. Years ago I had lost a child in a miscarriage, so we knew very well that this child too could leave for Heaven. The children seemed very concerned. They didn't know how to face me, and for a while they even stayed away from my room. I realized how frightened they were and I knew I had to continue to put aside my own fears in the hope of restoring their peace. One by one, they began to appear in my room. Each one showed me his or her own love and concern. I was surrounded by such an atmosphere of love that I began to experience great peace myself.

The next day Nick and I went together for my appointment. The bleeding had stopped and we were hopeful that this was a good sign. Still, it took a constant effort to keep trusting in God's love and to remain willing to accept his plan for us. The moment to take the ultrasound finally came and we were elated to watch the tiny child on the screen, heart beating and doing turns. Once again we had something beautiful to share with our children. We took it to be another opportunity that God was providing for us to be united as a family. As soon as the children came home from school that day, we showed them the pictures of their new brother or sister in the womb, as tiny as a thumb. They were all relieved.

As the months passed, the children followed the baby's progress very closely. We looked at books together, talked about development and size, and we remembered the baby in our prayers every night. When the baby started moving noticeably, they enjoyed answering each thrust with a little push of their own. They also liked to speak aloud to the baby knowing that they could be heard.

As the time of birth drew closer, everyone became impatient. "Isn't the baby ever going to come?" "Will the baby be born tonight, Mom?" Finally one night I left for the hospital. The following morning the children left for school ready to tell everyone that the baby would come home that day. Were we all disappointed when I came home that noon no longer in labor, but still without a newborn!

Later that evening the labor did return. I awakened Nick so that he could help me time the contractions. Shortly afterwards, the pains seemed to come closer apart and were lasting longer. We kept track of them for an hour. I was becoming more uncomfortable, so I asked Nick if he thought it was time to go to the hospital. Thinking that this might be just another false alarm he suggested we time a few more contractions. On the next contraction, the bag of water broke and he immediately knew that we had to act fast. There was a flurry of activity; Nick called the paramedics, alerted my parents, and was about to help me down the stairs to meet the ambulance.

Well, the baby was in a hurry and we just made it back to my bed in time for the birth. Nick received the newborn child, too involved to notice whether it was a girl or a boy. The children in the meantime were sound asleep! The paramedics took care of me and the baby and announced that we had a new son, who we were ready to name David

Michael. We decided to wake each of the other children, so Nick went from room to room to gather them together. We were all so surprised at having been able to experience the baby's birth in such a family setting.

N. and E. S.

"PEOPLE EVENTUALLY DO GROW UP"

When it was time to apply to college, our two oldest children knew fairly well what they wanted to study. Their readiness helped them to get accepted into the school of their choice.

Our third child, on the other hand, fell into the more common pattern of not really having any idea what to do, except that he *did* want to go to college. To compound the problem, he had not been a particularly good student. In spite of having an above average intelligence, his show of effort was minimal. Over the years we tried all the suggested tactics for turning him around. My husband and I even tried assuming different roles. I would try to be strict with him, while my husband more accepting, but to no avail. All of a sudden he was a senior, and we wondered how he was going to manage. I was concerned about how disappointed he would be if he didn't succeed in going to a school he might prefer. I tried to make him see his possibilities realistically, based on his record, while not wanting to put him down. I found myself constantly biting my tongue, so as not to say something hurtful, even when I saw his lazy behavior continue.

At about this time, my husband and I remembered that a friend of ours does pre-college counseling. We called him and he assured us he could help our son. During his visit, I remained at hand, but allowed my son to freely express himself, helping with responses only when he asked. (This was hard for me, because I felt so strongly that I could "help" by adding my own thoughts to the total picture.) Later, my son commented on my attitude during the session, saying he was surprised at how quiet I was. I had the impression it was a pleasant surprise.

After the session, he applied to about ten colleges, most of which were suggested by the counselor. He began to have a more positive attitude about himself, because they were not mediocre schools.

As important as the final decision might be, what was of still greater value was our new relationship. I recently told my son how I will sincerely miss him next year, as we have become so close during this difficult period. He gave me a genuine smile and said, "Well, Mom, I guess people eventually do start to grow up. Thanks." And with that my undemonstrative young man gave me a big hug.

T. Y.

"FORTY YEARS, WOULD YOU BELIEVE IT?"

Until a year ago, my son was living with a young woman and they were both drinking and using drugs. Over the years while they were together, my anger and frustration prevented me from having a close relationship with them. Our "dialogues" always consisted in my trying to impose my values onto them and in one way or another run their lives. Every attempt I made ended up on a negative note. During this time, they had a child. However, after about a year of difficulty in their own relationship, my son decided to return home.

As time went by, I became more and more aware of the undesirable environment that my grandson was living in. This made me furious, and I blamed his mother. When I had a confrontation with her one afternoon, I accused her of many things, which left both of us very bitter. After returning home, I felt the guilt of having treated her in such a way, but I also kept justifying it because of my concern for my grandson. A little voice kept haunting me to call her and be reconciled, but my feelings kept getting in the way. I finally did get the courage to call her, though I was very uncertain what her response would be. Perhaps she would just hang up. I told her how sorry I was. She listened attentively and told me how she too had wanted to apologize to me. We seemed to have made a new start.

A few weeks passed and I found out that she was about to move away in order to pursue a life of her own. My feelings of resentment came back to life once again. This time I no longer wanted to have anything to do with her. My only concern was my grandson. Since she and my son were not married, the child would become a ward of the state. Within me, however, I kept hearing the words, "As often as you did it for the least of my brothers, you did it for me" (Mt 25:40). I knew I had to convert, and accept her for who she was, no matter what happened to my grandchild. One day I went to visit her and it was like seeing her with new eyes. At the end of my visit she cried and we embraced one another. I no longer felt the need to lecture her or tell her how to run her life. While I was with her, she brought up the subject of my grandchild, and asked me if my son could take care of him for her. She even gave him legal temporary custody.

At this point my grandson moved in with me and his father. I felt that this was the hundredfold that we received, the fruit of loving to the end. The difficulties, however, were not yet over. Both my son and my daughter were wanted by the police. When the detectives would call me from time to time, I would make up a story and shield them. This had actually been going on for quite a long time. Although I felt what I was doing was wrong, I was their mother and I just could not bring myself to turn them in. I was torn as to what direction to take.

Trying to maintain a relationship with my husband and with each of my children often became very draining and overwhelming. It was a very difficult and painful situation, which humanly speaking I would run away from. It was my unity with other families around me that continually gave me the strength to keep renewing my love for my family. Because of my grandson, I seemed to have more opportunities to speak with my son, his father. I tried to listen more openly to him without judging him. The most difficult part of trying to dialogue was to not become impatient or disappointed due to a lack of response on his part. I kept renewing my love for Jesus on the cross, who had felt abandoned himself. He was the foundation of my rapport with my family. In moments of openness I encouraged my son to stop running and to pay his debt to society. Even though he didn't take the step to do it, I had the impression that something of the truth remained each time we talked.

I realized that hiding them in my home was against the law, and by now I felt more certain that it was not God's will to continue on like this. I felt at peace with this understanding, but at the same time, as a mother, I found putting it into action much more difficult. My heart was being crushed; it was so hard to put God first. I feared that if I turned them in, my husband would get very angry with me. I knew he and my children would never understand the action I felt I had to take. They would feel betrayed and probably end up hating me, yet I also knew I had to take the risk. I entrusted everything to God and his mercy even though I did not know how I could bring this situation to a peaceful end.

The next day while I was at work, the detectives came to my house and my husband let them in. Only my son was at home. To my surprise, I learned that he came out into the living room and willingly turned himself in. When I returned home my husband told me what happened and he was very peaceful. I could hardly believe what I was hearing. When I spoke later on to my son, he too, was at peace. He even told me, "You were right, Mom, I can't keep on running." I believe that my choice of God became the light that enabled my son to make his choice.

Meanwhile, for my daughter the solution did not come quite as fast. A few days later, I got another call concerning her. Remembering my decision, I told the detective that she was at home. I offered the telephone to her, but she left the house and didn't return again. After that, whenever the detective called, I really had to say that I had no idea where she was. My relationship with my daughter became very strained. Her attitude toward me turned very negative. Whenever I tried to talk to her, she rejected me. It was difficult to remain detached from my feelings, and difficult not to become altogether indifferent. I tried over and over again to reach out to her, but more often than not, all I could do was to pray for her.

One day, while driving, she was stopped by the police and arrested. She called from prison to let us know. I tried to talk to her, but there was no response. I wrote to her frequently and continued to pray for her constantly, always hoping that something would turn her around.

Some time later, my prayers seemed to have been answered. She called me from prison again. Her whole attitude toward me was different. She was gentle and loving, telling me that she was in a good program and that she felt the desire to receive Holy Communion. She had gone to confession earlier that day, for the first time in sixteen years. "You won't believe this, Mom," she told me, "but I even read the Bible and I'm going once a week to participate in a religious group discussion." I was very happy for her. God is a loving Father and my daughter's return to the sacraments was a miracle as far as I'm concerned.

I also see the fruit of living the gospel in my relationship with my husband. He is physically and emotionally a very sick man, and yet he is very sensitive to love. Recently, we had our fortieth anniversary. I didn't even know if my husband would remember it. That afternoon while I was at work, I turned around and there he was. He had brought me a beautiful corsage of roses. Inside there was a little card with a man coming out of a dog house and it said, "Forty years, would you believe it? You are still so tolerant and loving. God bless you."

All my married life I lived waiting for the situation to change, or for my husband and children to change. Instead, living the gospel is changing me. As I learn new values and try to live them, they affect my family as well. We all have learned, I think, how suffering can be transformed into love.

S. M.

NO GUARANTEES ON TOMORROW

Two months ago I went to my doctor because I was being bothered by a very minor medical problem. I'm normally such a healthy person that I didn't realize how long it had been since my last visit. In the light of this, my doctor wanted to do a full check-up and this lead to the discovery of a very large mass of tumor.

He immediately expressed concern and wanted me to follow it up with some tests. The serious tone of his voice which implored me to proceed with these tests made me understand, almost as if by instinct, that I had cancer.

I took the tests that the doctors suggested, and the report came back that the tumor was highly suspicious. I knew that I would have to find a good surgeon.

The next day I found myself driving alone into New York to have my X-rays read and to receive the official diagnosis. As I was driving along, a sense of fear welled up inside of me. I felt like I was going to the surgeon's office in order to receive a death sentence. I did receive confirmation that I had a cancer that must be surgically removed. It was a very difficult moment, but the first thing that came to mind was to renew my faith in God's love. There had been a time in my life when, if unpleasant things happened, I would question God's personal love for me. I was thankful that I no longer viewed life in this way. I was certain of his promise to be with us, with me, through anything. Thus I knew that if I could really accept him in this suffering, I would be united to him in a very special way. I realized that the wisest thing for me to do was to surrender to his loving plan. This immediately filled me with joy and peace, and fear disappeared.

The moment had arrived to communicate the news to our five children. The experience that day had given me a new freedom to love. Together with my husband I shared the news of my illness with them in such a way that they too saw everything as God's love for us. We felt closer than ever.

A few days later I was travelling back to the city again, this time by train with my husband. It was a long day, with many tests and consultations. Coming home exhausted that evening, I started to feel downcast, and fear returned. I repeated over and over to myself, "I believe in God's love for me." As we were about to get off the train I said to my husband, "You know I'm so drained from this day, I'm tempted to just go home, go to my room, lock the door and have a good cry." Then remembering my decision, I smiled and said, "Or I could make dinner for you and the kids." We laughed.

Well, God had another plan for us that evening. When we got home, our eleven-year-old daughter came hobbling to the door to show us her swollen ankle. We had to bring her to the emergency room right away. As we got back into the car I couldn't help thinking that this was getting ridiculous. I was supposed to go to the hospital four days later and now my daughter had a broken leg. Another conviction was stronger however, that again everything was an expression of God's love for me. This conviction seemed to be contagious. My daughter surprised me with an attitude free of complaints; she was even happy thinking that she too had a suffering that could be offered out of love.

My surgery went smoothly. In fact, the surgeon (I don't think he knew how many people were praying) kept saying how well everything had gone. However, we still had to wait for the pathology report as there was concern that, due to the size of the tumor, the cancer may have spread to the lymph nodes. This was the crucial point because it could indicate how long my life could continue.

Up to this point I thought I had given my life to God, but now it seemed as if I wanted to repossess it. It was a struggle to say another complete yes. Naturally, I gave him my preference, saying, "If nothing else Lord, my family does seem to need me," but I knew that I had to say yes to whatever his will for me might be and entrust my family to him. It was a much harder yes, but once I was able to say it I felt a great inner peace.

In the end we were happy and grateful to be told that the cancer had spread to only one lymph node. The oncologist (the specialist in chemotherapy) explained that a microscopic cell may escape and therefore chemotherapy is necessary. He then gently explained to me that people become very anxious because there are no guarantees. I didn't find this news depressing, because it was now a reality for me that there are never guarantees on tomorrow; there is only the present moment to be lived for God. Later, I learned that due to chemical changes in my body, I would not need chemotherapy at all. I felt immense gratitude to God for the gift of his very personal love throughout this entire experience, which above all, brought me closer to him.

U. L.

* * *

Living according to the gospel is living and teaching as Jesus did, as the Holy Family, Jesus, Mary, and Joseph did in the home at Nazareth.

We note in the experiences given the need for harmony, in the physical arrangement as well as the union of hearts. There is need for forgiveness—being the first to forgive and to reach out. The silence noted in one experience, the waiting, certainly must have characterized the home at Nazareth.

And, then, there is the need to say yes always, and with joy, to the will of God, as expressed in very ordinary ways, even when this means acceptance of the Cross.

Chiara Lubich once told her companions that our daily living out of the gospel should be such that observers, non-Christians, could rewrite the gospels from the observance of the way we live. And, so, these experiences of trying to live the gospel are recorded as testimony of ordinary folks, living as family, modeled on gospel values.

PART TWO:
TEACHING AS JESUS DID THROUGH THE UNITY OF THE FAMILY

Jesus educates by passing on to his disciples his teaching, especially, "This is my commandment: that you love one another, as I have loved you" (Jn 15:12). And, this is repeated again, in the fashion of the good teacher: "I give you a new commandment: Love one another. Such as my love has been for you, so must your love be for each other. This is how all will know you for my disciples: your love for one another" (Jn 13:34-35). In the unity of the family, having been reborn in Baptism, the child learns that he or she does not live in isolation from others but is a member of a family, a new and larger family, the Christian community. We are joined to others in common faith, hope and love.

This sense of oneness, of unity, is at the heart of Christian education as a concept to live, not simply to be taught. "Formed by this experience, they [the children] are better able to build community in their families, their places of work, their neighborhoods, their nation, their world" (TTJD #23).

Attempting to live in this way, moment by moment of each day, brings reciprocal richness to the parents and to the children. The bishops stated this: "In the family children learn to believe what their parents' words and example teach about God, and parents enrich their own faith by participating in the formal religious education of their children" (TTJD #25).

The experiences which follow will illustrate ways of doing this.

LOVE AND FIRMNESS

I have been living through our first emotionally difficult month with our nine-year-old son, Joseph. We live in an area where most of his school friends can buy more games and toys than we are able to afford. Our son knows that we love him and we do what we can, according to what we see to be God's will for each child and for the whole family. Yet, he would like to keep up with every new acquisition of his closest friends. There are also TV shows he would like to see that are truly not suitable for his age and are unacceptable even for us, his parents.

He has been learning to live our Christian values with us, and this is the first long period of time in which he has been struggling to truly make them his own personal values and decisions. Although he too wants to live in God's will, the pressure to keep up with his friends is very strong. His friends are not asking him to keep up with them; it is Joseph who feels he must do so.

During the first week, I patiently tended to him every day when he returned from school and went into the long list of what he wanted, when and why he wanted them. I knew I should listen and also explain to him our values as well as the family needs which our budget must meet.

By the second week, he stopped asking for the electronic games and focused in on new packs of football cards so that he could trade them at school every day. I felt his struggle more intensely and I really tried to understand his feelings. But my answer still had to be no, and a strain began to develop between us. It was very unpleasant to rehash every day the same problem. Only by recognizing this as the Cross I was called to carry, did I have the courage to face each new discussion.

The third week found me struggling to keep my patience. It was clear to me that all of my human reasoning and explanations were not getting through to him. I was sure that only my love and firmness in not giving in to him would be able to guide him to see in his situation what God wanted from him. When I had to say no to purchasing the football cards, my son got very angry and banged the wall. My husband Steve was home and he called Joseph over to talk with him. Glancing at each other, we renewed our "pact" of mutual love so that Jesus would be present in our midst (cf. Mt 18:20), and that Joseph would have the light and the peace to go through his struggle. He sat and spoke with us and he listened very patiently, but more to his father than to me. We shared our experiences of how we too have had to deny ourselves but when I mentioned this he looked at me angrily and said, "but that's only when you want big things!" I was then able to answer him saying, "No, it is also when I had to deny myself some very little things, perhaps a pair of shoes, or something I wanted like a chocolate bar which was not necessary at that moment, because the money should have gone for a bottle of milk." He turned back to his father and little by little he was able to examine some of his own desires. He and Steve seemed to establish a very good rapport.

As for myself, on one hand I felt rejected, while on the other I was happy to see that he was receiving the light to realize that some of the things he wanted were a little foolish.

Finally, he overcame his moodiness, thanked his father and even said he was sorry for having banged on the wall. But he purposely kept his eyes from me. At that moment

I felt deeply hurt. His joy could not be shared with me; I was still rejected.

I knew that God's will was to go beyond this suffering and to see Joseph with "new eyes" each moment.

Steve and I sat speaking a little while longer and then suddenly I felt Joseph's little arms around the back of my neck; he put his head on my shoulders and said with a big smile, "I love you, Mamma."

During the following days he slowly returned to be the child I had known earlier, the one who didn't consider football cards as the first thing in his life. Our rapport became more beautiful and deeper than before.

B. T.

GOD HAS GIVEN US A GIFT

About six months ago I began to realize that my parents, who are in their nineties, were going to need special help to carry on with their lives. Although my mother was pretty strong, my father was getting progressively weaker and I could see it was taking a toll on my mother. I wanted to respond to their needs, but the thought of taking on this responsibility frightened me. I also knew that with time their needs would only become greater. When I spoke to my sisters and brothers, it was obvious to me that they too were experiencing the same fears, because no one took the initiative to offer any concrete help. In my heart I knew I was being called to go beyond my fears, to be open to God's will in this situation.

Frank and I sat down to discuss this whole situation together and we agreed to go ahead to help my parents and to trust in God's love for all of us.

I made arrangements for a home health-aide to come in for a few hours every day and we took turns sleeping over at my parent's house because my father began to get disoriented at night and my mother was getting anxiety attacks.

On the day after Christmas, my father suffered a mild stroke while visiting my sister. Clearly they could not remain alone at home any longer. Once again I became afraid of what might lie ahead. I reminded myself that nothing happens without God's knowledge and permission and this gave me the courage to say another yes. So we moved my parents into our home.

After thirty years, I was living with my parents again. With the exception of some days when he would become withdrawn and confused, my father's spirits were good and he often made us laugh with some of the quick remarks he'd make. My mother, on the other hand, being fully aware of all that was happening, was now faced with some of the most difficult decisions of her life. The next day she would tell me that she prayed the Rosary and asked Mary to help her find peace. After ninety years, she was being asked to let go of everything: her husband, her security, her home, her health and independence; in short, her whole life. All that remained for her was to trust in God.

It was time for me to become a mother to my own mother. But that was easier said than done. I discovered this the first time we decided to cook dinner together. We were trying to make soup and we couldn't agree on anything, not even the size of the carrots and celery, or how much water to add. I wanted a slow simmer for one hour and my Mom wanted a rapid boil for two hours. I couldn't always make it to let go of my ideas and there were times when the best I could do was to bear the cost silently, so as not to do something that I knew was not love for her.

Besides all the activity involved with caring for my parents, we were in the middle of planning for my daughter's wedding and also dealing with serious business problems. Despite all these struggles, people would often comment that there was such a peaceful atmosphere in our home. This was always beautiful to hear because it made me aware that Jesus was present among us. I remember hearing once that the presence of Jesus is like good health; you don't notice it until it is gone.

One of the most painful moments my husband and I suffered during those months was the day we had a terrible argument. The unity we shared was broken. We both felt kind of dead that day and everything seemed to lose meaning for us. It showed us how important it was to maintain our unity at all costs.

In many ways my parents were a gift to the entire family. It was beautiful to see everyone including the grandchildren go beyond themselves in order to help in some way. I knew that some of my brothers were avoiding to come by because they would have found it too hard to face the reality that our parents' last years were upon us. Knowing this, I tried to find ways to encourage them to get involved in order to help them overcome their fears and take advantage of these precious moments we had left to share. Even though I could manage chores and errands on my own, I would often use these as excuses to ask them to come over and stay with my parents. For example, I called one brother reassuring him that Pop was really O.K. but that I needed his help to get Pop into bed. I know he was very happy that night because in taking care of my father, he forgot about himself and his fears. This was also true for another brother who was upset at the thought that my father might not recognize him. I called him one afternoon asking him to stay with our parents because I had an appointment elsewhere. When my brother arrived, my father not only recognized him, he gave him a wonderful greeting and hug. My brother was touched by this and left that afternoon a lot more free and peaceful.

Until my father's stroke, my mother would bathe him, but now that this was no longer possible, it became necessary for me to do it. The thought of having to wash my father was very upsetting to me. I called one of my sisters to ask her for her help. She happened to come on a morning when all I could think about were the mixed emotions running through me. I felt so uncomfortable. At one point my sister remarked about how difficult it must be for my father not to be able to care for himself and to have his daughters washing him. She helped me realize that I was thinking only of myself. I was very touched by her compassion for my father and the tender expression on her face as she cared for him. Her love brought my attention to Mary's love for Jesus, and I felt gently reminded to make a new effort, to start again.

My sister and I don't usually discuss spiritual things, but I felt prompted to tell her my impression. I told her she was a reflection of Mary to me. She was so moved; it was a strong moment of unity between us that we will always remember.

After a few months it seemed that things were under control.

Perhaps this was the reason my family felt it no longer necessary to call or visit as much. Perhaps they were trying to find the balance between being helpful and knowing when they were only adding to the confusion. My parents' needs did become greater, and most of the responsibility fell on myself and Frank. I started to feel abandoned and there were moments when I wanted my brothers and sisters to acknowledge the sacrifice we were making. We were becoming very tired and it was hard for me to be patient with my mother because I sometimes saw her as an obstacle. What helped me was to remember that while it was hard for me to give up my chicken soup, my mother was being asked to give up everything. Frank and I intensified our unity with each other, continually renewing our trust in God's love, each time gaining the courage to start loving again in the present moment.

As I look back on the past months I see now that God was teaching me something important. He was calling me to love my family in his way and not to look for any consolation, not to expect anything, not to be understood or comforted or supported by my leaning on the others, but to keep loving. This new understanding helped me to accept the others as they are and to realize that they also have their limitations. This freed me to love them and to stop judging them. I feel a great freedom and joy as I look back on how the unity in our family has grown through this experience—God has given us a gift.

R. R.

AN EARLY START

Since I had been late several times in the past weeks, one morning I was determined to get to work on time. So, when the alarm rang at 6:30, I turned it off and immediately began to prepare for work. It had previously been a habit of mine to stay in bed for a quick snooze until seven. But this morning, I wanted to make a good start.

My wife works two days a week, so at a certain point I called her to get up and prepare for work too. Our usual pattern was for me to drop her off at the train station, then take our baby to the babysitter, and finally drive to work. This day I really was determined to get everything ready and leave the house at 7:30. So far, we had made a good start.

Most of the times, I take a sandwich to school, while my wife picks something up at work. I remembered that my love should not be empty words, but be translated into action. So, I decided to prepare a special lunch for my wife. Usually I make something simple, like a peanut-butter sandwich, which takes only a minute to prepare. That morning I decided to prepare tuna on rye, my wife's favorite sandwich. Though it would require a little extra time, I thought I could manage. Just before leaving, I also tried to remember if we had packed everything we needed for the baby: diapers, toys, and her cup. Then I carried her portable crib and other things out to the car. When I got back inside, I picked up the baby in my arms, and waited for my wife to get ready.

I realized now that holding the baby in my arms was the signal to my wife that I was ready to go. She was not, and I waited there with my heavy winter coat on, still holding onto the baby. As the minutes passed, I felt more and more tired. At the same time, my desire to love was weakening too. I started imagining that I was going to be late again, and became worried that my supervisor would take this occasion to say something about my overall lateness. My pride was threatened, and it was this pride that began to get in the way of my decision to love concretely.

Of course, this kind of worrying and thinking began to build up inside. When I noticed my wife having trouble finding the token she needed for the train, I felt like I was about to explode. We got into the car and I drove my wife to the station. She could tell by my silence and the expression on my face that something was wrong. She opened the door and I finally did explode at her: "Get out, you made me late again."

When I turned the corner, I realized what I had just done. I felt miserable. I had failed terribly. This was not my first failure, but just the same, it was not a small matter either. I knew that my past failures have taught me that the best thing to do in this case is to make the decision to begin loving again, right away, and without trying to find some kind of justification for my action. I wanted to turn the car around and catch up with my wife to apologize to her. But chances were too slim that I would find her. Though I tried to call her from the office, I didn't reach her. My only alternative was to apologize face to face, when I would meet her later on.

That night, I explained to her how I had failed and how I had started again. She understood my experience very well, because she had gone through this process of growing many times herself. It was beautiful to start again together.

J. W.

GOD'S UNFORESEEN PROVIDENCE

Rick: Slightly over five years ago, because of a matter of principle, I resigned my job. The house we lived in came with the job, so we found ourselves without a home and only one month to find another one. At that time our youngest of six children was just six weeks old. We felt that it was important to stay in the area as our parents, grandparents and other relatives were close by. Before this job, we had been away from the family for some time. Our children were beginning to get a feel of their roots. Mostly, we felt it was God's will.

We began the process of looking for a new job and finding a new home. Since we live in a rural area and because of my unemployment, our possibilities of finding housing were limited. In staying open to God's plan for us, we looked at many houses to either rent or buy. Needless to say we were very concerned about this situation and had to repeatedly remind ourselves of God's own concern and Providence. We were looking and looking. With two weeks left before we had to move out, we went to look at a house in a nearby town. It didn't turn out to be the kind of house we needed. It was very nice but too small. However, next door was a larger home also for sale. From what we could see it was in need of a lot of work, but we made arrangements to see it. We took all the kids and Kim's grandma along with us. We weren't in the house five minutes when all of us felt that this was it.

Kim: Days later, I was back at the house again and realized that I had to be ready to lose it! While it seemed so right and we were doing everything we could to arrange financing for the house, it appeared an impossible situation. Once again it became very clear that it was in God's hands. To our great surprise, shortly after our giving it back to God, the realtor suggested a possible contract sale. One phone call to the owner and it was arranged. In our eyes, God had done the extraordinary.

Rick: While searching for a job, I had explored several options, including self-employment, yet nothing seemed to develop. Finally, there came an unexpected phone call from my present employer to whom I had not even made a job application, as I was unaware that there was even an opening!

Kim: Our family has seen God manifest his Providence in concrete ways that are not only unique and extraordinary, but also humorous and dealing with the very ordinary. Buying groceries for a large family can be quite a task, especially on a tight budget. We decided together to use the money we had on food that was nutritional. There was no room for snack food, outside entertainment, or soda pop. It seemed like we were constantly saying no to "can I go?" or "can I have?" because we just didn't have the money. Our primary source of entertainment was playing games with the children or watching TV together. At a certain point though, after several months, we began to hear some questions like, "Can't we even have a snack while we watch TV?" We began to get a little concerned because we didn't know exactly how this was affecting the children. Rick and I then decided that we should plan a little party. We would include some chips in the weekly shopping list, trusting that if we did it out of love, this wouldn't be the starting point of losing sight of our budget. Rick and our son Matt went out to do the shopping.

When they arrived home, Matt came in carrying a huge cardboard box. A little surprised, I asked what was in the box.

Matt answered "chips." In the box I counted eleven large bags of chips! I thought Rick had really gone overboard. After asking them where they got them from, Matt simply answered, "on the road." I found out what "on the road" meant. While they were driving, they had noticed several cars swerving around "something." They stopped to see what it was and discovered this case of chips. It had evidently fallen off a delivery truck. Not only did we have plenty for now and later, but also enough to share with others in the neighborhood. We had received the hundredfold we felt in trying to love our children in the way they needed it at the time.

The economic realities that we have faced as a family over the past several years have not always been easy to deal with. We have experienced, however, that God's love is such that his Providence comes in the ways in which we need it most, and in ways that touch the whole family and many others. We are reminded that the words of God are always so true, "Seek first his kingship over you . . . and all these things will be given you besides" (Mt 6:33).

R. and K. H.

A STIMULATING LEARNING ENVIRONMENT

My husband, Tim, and I have three children: Paul, who is seven; Anne, four; and Erika, two. We both are teachers. We realize that we must do everything possible to provide a stimulating yet wholesome learning environment for our children. One of the big issues that this includes is television.

Sometimes we have the temptation to just get rid of it, so as to avoid all the difficulties and challenges that it introduces into our lives. But we know that God put us here to live in the twentieth century; this is a phenomenon, we feel, which will not go away simply by ignoring it. Consequently, we have adopted our own set of tactics regarding television use. First of all, we decided to place it in an out-of-the-way corner of the house. This makes us more aware of the choice we are making when we do go to watch it. Then, we created a more convenient area for the children to play their games, to do art projects, listen to recordings, or to read, whether alone, together, or with other friends. At the beginning of the week we all sit down together to select television programs in advance and to schedule the week's viewing. Because the television is such an attraction—especially for the oldest—we have the children earn viewing time by doing family chores or by participating in other activities. When we can, we watch a program with them, and take out time afterwards to discuss what we have seen.

What we have found important is to encourage them to question the claims that are made—especially those in advertising—because children, we realize, tend to take everything on television as having special authority. We were pleased the other day when Paul turned to us at supper and said, "Is it true that the stains come out of the carpet right away, like they say in the commercial?"

As our children began to approach school age, we had to face another dimension of this challenge of nurturing our children's intellect with love. At home, we have a great deal of control over the experiences which they face; but at school, naturally, they must deal with the entire day on their own.

Even though our son Paul attended kindergarten, we did not become aware of the many circumstances he would face in first grade, until the school year had begun. We discovered, for example, that the students were "tracked" into various groups based on the scores of a reading test given at the end of kindergarten. We also discovered that the children would rotate during the day among several different teachers, who taught different subjects. From our own professional experience, we disapproved of these methods, but we also realized that such systems cannot be easily modified. There is little the individual teacher or the principal can do about them.

Nevertheless, during the course of the school year, we tried to find solutions to each of the various problems that have developed. On one occasion, Paul was experiencing difficulty in picking up certain reading skills, and in establishing relationships with his other classmates. To help him, we first tried to break down his problems into small manageable tasks. We helped him devise strategies to "breaking the ice" with the other boys and girls. Each morning, for example, we set a goal together of how many people he would attempt to begin a conversation with. As for his reading, we bought some extra material in phonics, and gave him homework to do from them. We didn't want these extra assignments to be a burden for him, so we created special awards for doing them, such as contributions to a toy fund or television time.

We also approached the teacher with whom Paul spends more time than the others. We asked her what her own perceptions were, and if she had any suggestions. On our part, we explained the problems that we saw, and how we were trying to solve them together with our son. As we spoke further, we even had the chance to share what our own concept of education is. She was very cooperative with us and began to work with him along the same lines. She too, began to encourage him to interact with the other children, and to make a point to the children that they all must respect one another.

Some time later, when Paul received his scores on another reading level test, the reading specialist remarked, "Where has this boy been all year?" as if looking for an explanation to why he improved so much since his entrance levels. In addition to that, the teacher now sends students with questions about their work to Paul, because he can usually help them solve their problems. We thought it so interesting that this is also giving him the chance to develop friendships as well.

Because his reading scores showed such improvement, he became eligible to transfer over to another teacher's group. But his present teacher suggested that he remain with her, so that she could continue to give him the attention he needed. She realized that such a cohesive atmosphere had developed among the children of her group that Paul would be better off staying where he was.

T. and J. M.

A CHOICE OF LIFE

I am a nurse by profession, and a housewife. My husband, Ken, and I, in raising our family, faced many challenges together. Now we were presented with a new one.

In January, when I was in the beginning of my second trimester of pregnancy, I received a call from my obstetrician informing me about the result of a screening test that she had done as part of a routine pregnancy blood work. This was a brand new screening test and I was not familiar with it at all. It had never been done during any of my other pregnancies. So I asked her what the significance of this test was—what the positive reading indicated, and what she was really so concerned about. She told me that this was a test to screen for neural tube defects in babies, which are defects in the spinal cord and brain, especially Spina Bifida. She suggested that I contact a genetic counselor whom she felt would be able to explain the test results in a clearer way to me and Ken.

I remember that as I was listening to her explain the implications of the test, I really wanted to just cry because, humanly speaking, I certainly wanted to have a perfect baby. But by the grace of God, in that present moment, I felt reminded of Jesus, who on the cross also felt abandoned and cried "My God, my God, why have you forsaken me?" (Mt 27:46). My past experience has lead me to look to him, especially in such trying moments, as if to tell him that I welcome the opportunity to be a little more like him, and that like him I would entrust my spirit to the hands of God. I knew I had to take this step once again, difficult as it was.

Ken was in Italy at the time and I was home with our nine children. I didn't even have Ken to share this suffering with, which was, I think, a grace too because I couldn't lean on anyone but Jesus himself. I said my yes, and entrusting my worries to him, I continued to try to live each present moment well, loving the children in whatever had to be done for them.

That same evening, I was scheduled to meet a group of close friends with whom I share my Christian journey. I had to remind myself that I was going there only to love the others, as I knew would be their own disposition, while at the same time knowing that it was important to share what I was going through. And so the opportunity did come to share it with one of my friends, and when I did, I felt that the burden I was bearing within me really became much lighter. I experienced a joy within me that I had never felt before. I was amazed at myself because I normally tend to hang on to worries rather than let go of them. Looking back, I know that such a joy and peace was the fruit of having tried to love Jesus in the way I mentioned before, and of experiencing that moment of unity with my friend, who shared my burden so completely. Putting everything in the heart of Jesus, we said that we would pray for whatever the will of God was, knowing that his will would be an expression of his love for me and my family.

I had to hold off for a week before making the appointment with the genetic counselor because I wanted to wait for Ken to come home from Italy.

When I called the genetic counselor's office for the appointment, and gave the secretary the information — the positive test results, that I was in my twentieth week of pregnancy, and so on — she seemed more than a little upset that I didn't call earlier. She wanted me to come the very same day but I told her that it didn't appear possible, but that I would be happy to come one day the following week. She spoke to the doctor for a moment, then came back on the phone to tell me that my situation involved a certain urgency, and that I should come immediately because the doctor may be required to terminate my pregnancy. In my case, she said, I didn't have much time to spare because abortions are only allowed until the twenty-fourth week of pregnancy and since it takes four weeks to get the results from the amniocentesis, I was really in trouble. I listened to what she had to tell me with as much love as I could and very calmly assured her that the next week's appointment would be fine since abortion was not an alternative for me. I merely wanted to see the counselor in order to be better informed and to find out how I could help my obstetrician assist the baby when delivery time came. So she reluctantly said, "O.K., it's your decision."

When the day came for the appointment, Ken and I renewed our unity with each other.

As the doctor spoke, it seemed to me that he was encouraging me to have an amniocentesis so that if the study showed that there was in fact something wrong with the baby, I could then have the pregnancy terminated. We assured him right away that we wouldn't have the baby aborted and that we were just interested in finding ways to help the baby whether he or she was deformed or not. Being a nurse, I was also aware of the risks involved in undergoing an amniocentesis both for myself and for the baby, although I was not up to date on the statistics. The doctor then told us that with a positive blood test, there was a one in 241 chance that we could have a baby with Spina Bifida. Without the positive blood test the chances are one in 2,000.

So then Ken asked him what the chances were of having a deformed baby from undergoing the amniocentesis and the doctor answered, "Oh, about a half percent," which sounded like there was an insignificant chance of harming the baby with the amniocentesis. We asked him what the chances were of having a spontaneous abortion with the amniocentesis. He agreed that this could happen but again minimized the significance of it. Then the doctor said, "Aren't you at least concerned about having an abnormal child because you're thirty-nine years old?" and I said "No." At this point, he took out a folder which contained the latest statistics on having an abnormal child when the mother is over thirty-five years old. I remember Ken saying that certainly having a defective baby was better than having no baby at all and that we knew a child who had Spina Bifida who was really beautiful, loving, and very bright. We then decided not to undergo the amniocentesis but gave thought to a sonogram which could be helpful but not harmful to the baby or myself.

As we were walking out of the hospital, we began to sort out some of the statistics he had given us, especially the ones comparing the chances of having a Spina Bifida baby, which was one in 241, and having a deformed baby from the amniocentesis, which was one half percent. In looking at the statistics closer, we realized that there was less than one half percent chance of having a Spina Bifida baby even with a positive blood test. This confirmed our feeling that the doctor was in fact giving information in a biased manner and in a way that would encourage mothers to undergo amniocentesis, increase their chances of having a deformed baby and also terminate their pregnancies. We decided that Ken should call the doctor back to ask him if we really understood him well and confront him with the fact that his presentation had been biased. The doctor agreed that we had understood him correctly and that he did present the statistics in a biased manner. He also said that in most cases, couples preferred to have either a perfect child or no child at all.

A day later, we spoke with our obstetrician and together we decided that we would do a sonogram but we would have to wait for at least two months until the baby was in a viable stage so that if there was a problem the obstetrician could then do a caesarean section and deliver the baby before the nerves to the baby's legs were damaged.

Needless to say, there were many moments during this waiting period that were difficult and my choice to continue to love Jesus in such a way had to be renewed over and over again. And each time I said yes, I experienced a joy inside which is difficult to describe. These were also weeks of discovering the countenance of Jesus in all those who are handicapped. As if by divine coincidence, I had met at this time a young man, who appeared to have cerebral palsy. We met at Mass in our parish church near my home. God, in his generosity, really gave me a gift through this young man. At first, each time I saw him, I would begin to feel sad, thinking that my baby may be faced with a similar condition as his own. One morning, however, while being in his company, I understood something important. In spite of his physical difficulties, he attended college. At Mass, he would pray for his family, for his friends who were going through their own personal difficulties, for those who were taking exams, and for those who assisted him so patiently. Through him, I rediscovered Jesus who was able to love his neighbor in spite of his handicap. Jesus too, I thought, continued to love us even when nailed to a cross. I understood, through this young man, that a handicap didn't stop a person from becoming a saint. This was really a consolation for me.

The day after Easter, Ken and I went to the hospital to

have the sonogram done and as far as we could see, the baby was perfect.

Today we have a healthy boy, and I am grateful for having chosen life in whatever way God chooses to give it, believing that his will is always his love for me.

H. M.

OUR THIRD CHILD

I was pregnant and overdue with my third child so my obstetrician sent me to the hospital for testing every other day to make sure the baby was O.K. One of the tests is an electrocardiogram that monitors the baby's heart beat. After taking the test the first two times, I had become familiar with the procedures, terminology and graphs.

The third time I went was early on a Monday morning when I was exactly two weeks past my due date. After a few minutes of monitoring, I noticed that the machine started going haywire. The nurse technician ran to my side and tried to find the baby's heartbeat with the stethoscope that's hooked up to the machine.

The problem was that with each movement the baby's heartbeat was dipping very low. I could tell by her face that the nurse was worried. After a couple of minutes, she called to a receptionist across the hall to get the doctors in there right away. In the meantime, the nurse continued to hold the stethoscope in place and track the baby's heartbeat which we saw being registered on the monitor. Her hands were trembling, and each time the monitor would show the heart rate dip to zero. She would quickly find it again and then tell me: "I've got it, I've found your baby's heartbeat, it's there!" The more she tried to reassure me, the more I realized how serious the situation was. I really felt scared and was afraid to move because I knew somehow it might cause the baby to move, and the monitor could lose his heart beat again. The obstetrician and some other doctors examined the graphs and charts that the monitor had made to see what had been happening. They told me that they were calling my own doctor and that he would probably come to deliver the baby right away.

I knew I had to live each moment well—to trust in God, to keep him first in my life, to accept whatever happened as a manifestation of his love. I also knew there was a real possibility of losing the baby and I was afraid. I felt that God wanted my *total* yes to his will, not a "yes God, I'll love you if you let the baby live," which would have been like bargaining out of desperation: but a "yes God, I accept whatever happens as your love for me, as your will."

I knew then that if we lost the baby, there would be tremendous pain and suffering, but there would not be a sense of abandonment by God. Even if I lost the baby, I knew Jesus would be present with his love. It was clear for me that I should remember him in his greatest suffering, when he too had felt abandoned.

This helped me to go beyond my own troubles and show concern for all the people around me—the nurses and doctors and my husband whom I had called to come to the hospital. He told me that he had called all our friends and that they were praying for me and the baby. Experiencing this loving community around me gave me more strength.

Throughout the labor there was constant concern by the doctors and nurses about the baby. In the end, however, everything turned out well. It was a powerful experience for my husband and me, which remained with us. We realized that due to our mutual love, which brought the presence of Jesus in our midst, we were always in peace, even during the most difficult moments. All our friends who had shared so much in our pain, shared then as much in our joy, thus multiplying it and making it deeper.

B. R.

WHY IS THIS HAPPENING TO US?

Martin: Elaine and I have been married for five years. We have a three-year-old daughter named Laura. At the end of last September, we learned that Elaine was expecting our second child who would be born at the end of May.

However, by the middle of December, although just four months pregnant, Elaine was experiencing complications. Most noticeable was the swelling of her feet. She visited the doctor but the swelling did not respond to the medication. She was therefore hospitalized for further testing. The results were frightening: the diagnosis was lupus which had attacked both kidneys. The malfunction of the kidneys had caused the swelling, which by now had spread throughout her body. She was considered a patient with a high risk pregnancy.

This new situation turned out to be very difficult for me. Along with all the practical things I needed to take care of, I was troubled by a question: why was this happening to us at such an early stage of our lives?

At that time I was working as a waiter; my five-day schedule also included weekends. My hours were from 5 P.M. to 1 A.M. Before Elaine was hospitalized, she was working as a kindergarten teacher from 8 A.M. to 3 P.M. So I spent the daytime with my daughter, but very little time at home with my wife. Now with Elaine in the hospital, there was no one to take care of our daughter while I was at work.

My worries were mounting, but at the same time I wanted to live this experience together with Elaine in the fullest way, believing in God's love for us. One of his answers seemed to be the arrival of her mother, who would stay for a few months to take care of our daughter during my working hours.

Elaine: When I discovered how seriously ill I was, I suddenly remembered what I have been asking Jesus all these years, that he take me before I would have the chance to leave him. I realize now how complacent I had become, and how taken up by the world. Now he seemed to be calling me back to be more faithful to him; to follow more closely his plan of love for me.

The doctors explained the state of my condition very clearly to me. I was very frightened at first, especially when they suggested that I terminate the pregnancy in order to save my own health, and perhaps my life. Only then could they begin to reconstruct the function of my kidneys. In their opinion the baby had very little chance to survive anyway, and he or she would only complicate, if not worsen my condition. The doctors explained what I would have to go through if we decided to keep the baby. It could mean a lifetime of renal hemo-dialysis.

Although this was so frightening, my answer still had to be no. By believing in God's love I was able to forget myself and live for the baby. The series of treatments began and I found myself under hemo-dialysis almost every day.

During this trying period however, I felt like I was not going through it alone. I felt that Mary was always near to make things sweeter. I discovered her greatness and her immense love for me. She was the Mother of God, but at the same time *my* mother. I never imagined being so close to her and I really wanted to return her love by living like she did.

Martin: While Elaine was in the hospital, my schedule became very hectic. All of a sudden I had become a father and a mother to our daughter who was still demanding a lot of attention. All the household chores were left up to me too, and sometimes when I was very tired, I was tempted to give up and to complain. But many times when our daughter would ask me something, I remembered, " . . . as often as you did it for one of my least brothers, you did it for me" (Mt 25:40), and that made my relationship with her change very much.

Elaine: After a month in the hospital, our baby was born but he only weighed about one pound because, at this point, I was only five months pregnant. He lived for little more than a day, enough time to baptize and confirm him. All this time I was ready to give my life for him and now it seemed he was giving his for me, since with his departure the doctors could now treat my kidneys. It was a great suffering because I saw, touched, played, and talked to him during that short time that he lived, but everything seemed to tell me that he deserved heaven, not earth.

As days went by, things didn't become any easier because I didn't know if I would be cured and be able to function without dialysis treatment. Each day was filled with unpleasant surprises: dialysis, blood transfusions, surgeries, needle sticks, cardiograms, and so on. Knowing what was ahead of me would make me anxious and afraid.

At this point I remembered Mary again. I realized that her greatness consisted in her many sufferings and in the way she lived through them. From then on, whenever I had to go through more tests and surgery, I would think of how Mary would react if she were in my place, and this gave me the strength to also love the people around me. One time the doctors had to perform three minor surgeries on my arm to put in a fistula that would be used for the dialysis. Although my arm was numbed, I started to feel pain at a certain point and the doctors explained that I would have to bear the pain since anesthesia could not be given inside the veins. The nurses around me told me, "Go ahead, scream and shout, we know it hurts." But instead I found myself praying until the surgery was over. This was one of the most beautiful things that happened to me during that time.

Martin: After several months Elaine finally got better and I found a new job with better working hours and a higher salary. I really saw this as a manifestation of God's love since this allowed me to spend more time with my family. God can never be outdone in generosity.

Elaine: I am alright now. Even though I still have lupus, which is for life, I am no longer on dialysis. My kidneys are "miraculously fine" to quote the doctors. All I keep praying for is to be able to live my life in such a way as to make it a little gift to Mary who was always with us.

E. and M. M.

TIME FOR THE FAMILY

Michelle: My husband, Dennis, and I have a thirteen-month-old daughter named Kaitlin. I am also a working mother, a computer-programmer. Recently, my company has been pressuring me to work overtime. My bosses often work late and respect employees who do the same. I felt a conflict within me because of this pressure. I saw employees hired at the same time I was, working twenty to thirty hours overtime, being enrolled in fast-track management training courses, being given promises of promotions, being taken out to lunch, and so on. A part of me really wanted to receive the same kinds of affirmation. I felt that if I worked the overtime hours, I would be seen as an employee with potential.

But another voice, deeper within me, seemed always to insist that there was another place for me during the evening hours and weekends. Near quitting time I would sit at my desk and think: "What does God want from me in this moment?" My conscience always told me: "It is time now to go home and be mother and wife to your family." And that is what I did.

Still, I was afraid because I thought that this would reflect in a negative way on my performance review. When the day arrived, however, my bosses welcomed me into their office with big smiles, handshakes, and lots of praise. And even after I told them that my family was my first priority, they gave me a salary increase twice the size of the one we agreed on when I first took the job. At first, I was flabbergasted, but afterward I felt a confirmation of two things: that the choices I made can be recognized as legitimate in the world of work, and that when I try to do the Father's will and not my own, the Father is also working, taking care of the rest.

Before we had Kaitlin, we didn't know whether we could afford to have a child because we had to pay off rather high debts every month for the loans we took to attend school. We knew we would be paying them for a long time. But communicating with other families helped Dennis and me to think more about what God's will was for our family. Together we realized that God did not want us to wait ten years to have our first child. We knew that we had to trust in his help and that he would provide for what we needed.

Ever since then, we have had continual and surprising Providence from God. For one thing, we never have had to worry about clothes for Kaitlin—we not only have enough, but an abundance of clothes and they keep coming in. When Kaitlin grew out of one size, we considered those clothes as surplus and we thought we should send them to a relative who just had a baby. This was hard because I loved those clothes and we did have a reason to keep them since we did intend to have more children. Still, we felt we should give them to those who needed them now. Within a few days, more clothes came in and we gave them away to a lady who needed small sizes and then, beyond our expectation, she gave us some clothes that were just what Kaitlin needed. It seemed that as soon as I gave some clothes away, right on the heels each time came more clothes. We really felt the love of God in all these circumstances.

Dennis: I am a counselor and supervisor of counselors who work at a Treatment Center for Juvenile Delinquents, ages fourteen to eighteen. Our job is to rehabilitate these young men who are admitted on charges of burglary, arson, rape, and assault. We try to teach them how to care about themselves and other people and to show them that they are valued and worth caring about. Then we help them get vocational training and jobs, which is an exhausting and time-consuming aspect of the whole program and which I am responsible for. This is in addition to my main job as supervisor of counselors. Often this lead me to work very long hours. On Mondays and Tuesdays, I usually didn't get home until eight or nine o'clock, and I would often go to work on Saturday or Sunday.

One evening, when I arrived home again at nine o'clock, Michelle tried to tell me about her day with Kaitlin. I was really trying to listen, but I couldn't help but doze off. Michelle was so tired of this nightly routine that she yelled at the top of her lungs, "You spend the best of you at work and Kaitlin and I only get what is left over, which isn't very much!" This hurt me a lot because I knew it was true. I became very angry because it seemed to me that either my work would suffer or my family would suffer, and either way someone would be disappointed in me.

Later, I realized that I wasn't doing God's will and would have to give up the career development sector of my job. This was really difficult and I would not have done it if I didn't think that God really wanted me to spend more time with my family. When I went to the Executive Director, it hurt me to say, "I can't handle both jobs anymore." He accepted my resignation from career development and I figured that he would now think less of me. But I had to try to be a better husband and father.

Several weeks later the Executive Director informed me that he was not going to allow me to resign from the career development work. Instead, he would give me twelve hours each week free from my supervisor's job to do career development, plus he would give me an assistant. To me, this was an act of God because the administration usually tries to get you to do more things without taking away anything you are already doing. I was completely overjoyed and thought, "Now, doesn't it say in scripture that if you renounce anything for his sake he will repay you a hundred times over?" (cf. Mt 19:29). I felt I had received the hundredfold.

Since that time I have been very deliberately keeping the number of hours I spend to about forty-five a week. By choosing to spend more time with my family, I felt that I was dropping out of the competition for promotion to the level of Program Director, which I had hoped to achieve. But recently I heard through the grapevine that my company is soon to begin a new program at a new facility and that I have been chosen to be its Program Director.

D. and M. M.

YES, OUT OF LOVE

Rose: For about four months our son, Jay, was very ill. We would go back and forth to doctors, but no one was able to diagnose his problem. As time went on, I became more and more worried. All kinds of things would come to mind and, over and over again, I would try to put them aside, and to concentrate on living the present moment well. Each day was a constant exercise to be faithful in the little things, because I was always tempted to stop and to dwell on my worries.

One day he had to return for more examinations and blood tests. The doctor sat us down and said the situation was improving, but that he had to be honest with us and say that there was a possibility of a terminal disease. My heart seemed to stop. I could not believe what he was telling us. Fear filled me and I was not able to listen any further to his words. Then, I remembered that in the doctor, too, there was Jesus to live for, so I immediately began to listen again, giving him all my attention. When I tried to forget myself, including my fears — when I tried to love again — I felt that a light filled my soul. I realized how difficult it was for the doctor to say these things, and I was able to be more concerned for what my son may have been feeling.

John: When I learned that our son might have a terminal disease, my first reaction was, "My God, we are trying to live a good, Christian life, and trying to give God everything, and yet this happens. . . . " Our family, which had been peaceful and serene, seemed to collapse. But then I realized that I had to put aside my own suffering in order to live for this boy, because he needed my love. I thought over how I could do this, and found that it was in little, simple ways, like spending time with him, making tea for him—all the concrete ways I could think of. I tried to live for him with all my strength, knowing that time, perhaps, could be short.

Rose: As the days passed, it grew even more difficult to put aside my worries, and to try to do God's will, to make the decision to believe in his love in everything. Each day, as I would do the housework, it seemed that everything became meaningless, and again my fear would return. Everything around me seemed to crumble. The only thing that made sense was to try to do each thing well, as an act of love, thinking that it is God's will to do the laundry, to prepare the meals, to answer the needs of my husband and our three other children.

The more I was able to trust in the love of God, the stronger became my faith that if I lived each moment like this, God would give me the grace to know how to lose this child, if it were his will.

At times, I wondered what I could say to my son; I had no words. I realized that in this moment, more than trying to do something concrete that could be an external expression of love, I had to simply *be* love. He belonged to God, and I believed that this was God's personal love for him, too. Our son remained calm and peaceful, and he told me, "I'm not going to worry. I'm just going to take it one moment at a time." In striving each moment to live like this throughout this period, I saw that he too was able to love and remain in the present moment.

John: We always tried to understand what could be God's will. At a certain point we had two doctors' opinions, both different. One doctor said, "Have a biopsy and have it checked." The other doctor was strictly against the operation to have the biopsy. You don't want to make a mistake with your son's life. I prayed about this with Rose, and we prayed as a family hoping to find what could be the best solution. He was already carrying this illness for several months, and his whole immune system was down; we knew he could not go on this way. In my heart I felt that he should have the operation, but I wasn't really sure. As it turned out, I had to take my twelve-year-old in for a check-up. The doctor happened to be the same one who had done the blood tests for Jay. In fact, the doctor even asked how he was doing. I explained the situation and how uncertain we were of what to do next. He then checked Jay's card and remarked, "Well, if his condition hasn't changed any, in my opinion, the doctor who suggested the operation is an excellent one. My heart told me this was a confirmation of what we had thought. I felt that this was God's will given to us through this set of circumstances and we took this direction sure of doing the right thing.

You can imagine our joy when the operation revealed only an infection concentrated in one area, and which the doctor was able to remove. After some time, our son was completely well. What remained in us was the experience of God's love when we try to follow him moment by moment.

J. & R. D.

* * *

The formative power of a Christian family, living in unity, *living a communitarian life, is essential to teaching as Jesus did.*

What unity must have characterized that home of Nazareth! Even to walk past the house must have given one a sense of holy ground, blessed by the unity of soul of the family living within.

Again, the ways of making this a reality today in our homes are simple. It is the small things which describe the values. This can be seen in the waiting of the mother in the first experience for the return of the son, certainly the pain of Mary while Jesus was away. It can be seen, not only in the bond with the children, but, as in the experience of "God Has Given Us a Gift," in the ever-changing faces of the relationship to aging parents and to the members of the extended family. The unity can only grow moment by moment, in openness to the expressions of God's plan, of "starting again together."

We are reminded in the experience of Rick and Kim that there are always surprises in the unfolding of God's plan. Often, the economic factors are uncontrollable and unpredictable. Out of the unity lived by the family comes the light to deal effectively with these factors. And, without notice, there come the joyful surprises and blessings of the Providence of God, which arrive at moments of greatest need.

This is the "learning environment" (as T. and J. M. have shared) in which teaching as Jesus did takes place. It should be the environment of every professional classroom and school. It is the atmosphere created by parents and teachers living the gospel in unity. We have a promise of this— "Wherever two or three are gathered in my name, there am I in their midst" (Mt 18:20).

Several of the experiences speak of suffering and of pain in the efforts to live in this way. On the other hand, the same experiences speak of receiving "the hundredfold." There might seem to be a paradox here to the person who may not have yet experienced the paradox of Good Friday and of Easter Sunday, the Cross and the Resurrection.

PART THREE:
TEACHING AS JESUS DID
IS SERVICE FOR OTHERS

The experience of unity in the family naturally leads to service of the others. "We should not live for ourselves," Chiara Lubich says, "we must live for the others, 'making ourselves one' with them in everything except sin." No human joy, no human sorrow is a matter of indifference to the community established by Jesus.

In today's world this requires that the Christian community be involved in seeking solutions to a host of complex problems such as poverty, war, racism, and environmental pollution.

In the pastoral letter, we see it stated in this way: "Christians render such service by prayer and worship and also by direct participation in the cause of social reform."

The unity of the family is the basis for this transformation. Through this education the children and the entire family become a small church, a dynamic reality open to society around it and to its needs, orienting the children especially to look beyond themselves, to others and their needs.

To live and to teach in the family in this way is possible, as the following experiences of families will indicate. They witness to the strength which grows from mutual love and goes out in service to others, building a new humanity.

SHARING

Brian: Lorraine and I try to instill in our children an attitude of sharing their belongings with each other and with others. We have tried to educate them in this regard, first of all, by sharing our own goods.

For example, we have a garage sale box in our basement closet. We hold a garage sale every year to help other families meet their needs. The children have noticed throughout the year that we put things in this box which are quite nice, but no longer useful. They decided to follow this practice and when they sort their things out, they often add some of their belongings to the box — to the point where we now have more children's items than adult's, and we are overflowing the closet.

As parents we find that we are not always the source of example in the family, for many times the children educate one another. During Halloween, for instance, we encourage the children to pour out their goodies into one common bowl, so that the candies they collected become the whole family's candies. Our youngest child, when she was four years old, found it difficult to accept this. She wanted to hold on to her own collection. But seeing how her older brothers accepted this as being a normal way of loving one another helped her to also share her goods.

Lorraine: Our family, just as other American families, has to struggle against the almost overwhelming consumerism of our society. There are times when it might seem very important for our kids to have certain designer clothes or want something that their friends might have. Sometimes, however, they surprise us by their generosity too. For example, one of our sons received two dollars from his grandfather on Christmas Eve. He had the money in his pocket during Mass. When it came time for the collection, he decided to put his two dollars in the collection basket as his Christmas gift to the Church. Interestingly enough, after our meal on Christmas day, my brother decided to treat my son to an instant lottery ticket and to my son's delight, he won two dollars.

As the children get older and start to earn money, we encourage them to broaden their vision and think of other people's needs also. Our son is a paper boy and earns a certain amount every week. Out of this sum, he keeps some spending money and gives an equal portion of his earnings to a group of young people who are working on a project to assist poor families. After hearing about a soup kitchen in New York City where his aunt works, he decided to give money for that as well.

B. and L. W.

THE CHOICE

"We have your son here in the emergency room. He has been in an accident."

It had been quite a night. My husband and I stayed up to watch the news and then prepared for bed. At eleven o'clock the phone rang; I tried to guess who it might be. Sleepily I answered. But the long distance message cleared my head immediately. Calmly I asked the nurse how badly he was hurt. "Lacerations on the face, leg and arm, and a compound fracture on the left forearm." "May I speak with him?" A few seconds passed. "Mom? I'm okay. They are taking me into surgery now. I'll call you later." His voice was strained with pain. The next morning he called again and explained what had happened. "The driver of the other car," he said, "was at fault when she did not give me the right-of-way, leaving me no alternative but to smash into the side of her car, fly into the air and fall on my left side. My helmet saved my life." He blamed the lady for everything. He said, in fact, "she blamed herself for the collision." He went on to say that if through her negligent driving she had ruined his chances for a career in aviation, she was going to pay.

I was silent.

Our son had worked hard to attain all his present ratings necessary to be a commercial pilot, which had been his dream since the seventh grade. Now, at the end of his college years, that dream might be destroyed depending on the extent and seriousness of his injuries. In the space of a second, a life's ambition is drastically changed because of the carelessness of one person. I could understand all that he was saying against this turn of events. However,

88

when his bitterness and vindictiveness were being spent on the person who was driving the other car, I really began to be concerned. This was not like him.

Later that evening, my husband placed a call to his hospital room. The conversation was the same; "Somebody's going to pay for this. She is not getting away with it." From what he went on to say, I knew his well-meaning friends were supporting his bitterness. But I had to understand them too, just as I had to understand the woman responsible. Yet I felt that there was still something else to be done. This vindictiveness was eating at my son. I really prayed hard and asked God to tell me what to do.

The next morning I decided to call him. It was a decision that proved to be an absolute agony for both of us. After I felt better assured about the status of his physical condition, I started speaking of the situation which was causing him so much anguish. He misunderstood. He believed I was defending the woman responsible for his injuries. "Please try to understand," I went on, "that she didn't mean to do it. You told me yourself how tormented and guilty she felt. You must put aside these bitter feelings now and start all over again. Try to shut out all those voices around you and listen to the voice of your own conscience."

He was very upset now, "Do you know what I look like? I'm bruised and broken. I can't walk because my leg is stiff and all stitched up, so is my face. My arm is in traction with two steel plates screwed into my bones to hold them in place. I may never fly. And you ask me not to be bitter towards her? I don't understand."

It was really painful.

"There are all kinds of injuries," I told him. "This woman may be going through her own private hell, her own kind of suffering. I thank God you are still alive. Do you think he spared you to be so unforgiving?" There was a long silence on the other end of the phone. Then, "Mom, you don't have to tell me that it is only through the grace of God that I'm alive. But I don't understand your attitude."

This additional suffering that I was inflicting on him was really agonizing. And it was killing me too, to know that my son was in a hospital two thousand miles away and with no one to comfort him.

Our phone call ended quietly. My hand still rested on the receiver as I silently placed my son in the hands of God. With renewed trust in God's love, I made the effort to take care of the things that had to be done around the house.

As the day wore on I was having second thoughts. Friends and relatives were calling asking about our son, and I began to detect the same tone of bitterness in some of their voices. One or two were downright vengeful. While my own husband agreed with me, he also defended the feelings of our son adding a few of his own. I was really troubled. Was I wrong? What right did I have to inflict this suffering on him? Shouldn't I have at least comforted him by seeming to agree with him? What had I done?

I prayed. I told God I did what I did because I loved my son, but it was a love that went beyond the love of a mother. I knew in my heart that if I were just a mother to him I would be like his friends and relatives who were harboring bitter feelings for the woman driver. But would I have loved the way the gospel suggests it? No! I had to do my part, step back and leave the rest up to God.

The next day a familiar voice was calling long distance. "Hiya Mom!" It was the relaxed voice of the son I had always known. "Well, you sound pretty good today," I said. "Yeah," was his reply. "They x-rayed my leg and it's not broken. I'm hungry; there's not enough to eat here.

The doctor says that I can go home in a week. By the way, the lady came to see me last night."

I didn't say a word.

He continued, "Yeah, she stayed for half an hour. That was pretty neat of her. I told her it took a lot of courage on her part. And Mom I wasn't mean or anything. In fact I made sure that also my friends wouldn't say the wrong thing to her while she was with us."

We went on about other things. But now he was free. The burden of revenge was gone, the weight of bitterness was lifted. How close I came to compromising. I thanked God for the grace to love to the end.

L. P.

THE GIFT OF FAITH

Our home is always open to other families. One of them which we had known for more than ten years was Ray and his wife and daughter. They came often to our home and shared in our desire to keep Jesus among us.

Some time ago, Ray had become very ill. As his illness progressed, it became more and more difficult for me to watch his condition get worse. I felt helpless, and knowing that I could not change his situation made it even more difficult.

When we first met Ray, he was an atheist and used to torment us with his request to prove that there really was a God. We rejoiced in the gift of faith he had later received. Now we found ourselves visiting him in the hospital. During our visits, we brought him the Eucharist and prayed with him. We, too, had to face the reality that God was calling him home and it was very painful. Yet, love seemed to cover over everything, including the sting of death. As his suffering deepened, Ray wanted only to be faithful to believing in the love of God for him in all things, and he would repeat over and over, "My Lord knows what he is doing."

Over the years, we had encountered many situations with their family and shared many joys and sufferings. During the period of Ray's illness, we watched so many fruits unfold. Ray's suffering was not in vain. His daughter who was away from the Church for many years came back. His son who did not want to know anything about God found himself praying with us on many occasions. His wife and another daughter seemed to mature in their outlook on what was happening. Both of them had great difficulty in coping with death in the past, and each one this time was saying her own heroic yes to God.

We received a phone call at 2:00 A.M., the night Ray died. It was his wife asking us to come over. When we arrived at their house, their twenty-two year-old son was on the front porch. He embraced us and said, "I love you people so much, you are really my family." Ray's wife was peaceful and there was a peace that seemed to be permeating the entire house.

Later they told us how our faithfulness in loving them over the years has always been a source of strength for them. I felt I had really served God in loving Ray to the end.

A. D.

THE END AND THE BEGINNING
OF A MARRIAGE

Billy: I grew up on the coast, where my parents had a flourishing business. I was an only son and up to the age of twenty-four I sailed through life with neither problems nor ideals. I led the sort of life that all young people in vacation resorts live, especially those with indulgent fathers and a bit of money. Then I met Julie.

Julie: I lost my parents when I was very young. There were no close relatives who could take care of me so I grew up in an orphanage. I picked up a job while I was still studying, but the pace was too much for me and I ended up exhausted. I was a bank clerk. One of the managers saw the state I was in, so he and his wife tried to help me by offering me their time and companionship. Through visiting them and their children I experienced the warmth of being part of a family. One day when I was particularly tense and tired, they said to me, "Look, take the keys to our cottage at the shore. Go there and try to pull yourself together, and don't come back until you are feeling better." It was the end of the winter. At the same time Billy, too, was at a loose end and we met each other one day as we were both wandering along the beach.

Billy: It really was "love at first sight." We decided to get married right away. Yet, I really hadn't understood anything about Julie, or about her life and her need for attention and warmth. As far as I was concerned, I loved her and thought that this was enough for her.

A year later, our first son was born by an emergency caesarean section. After only eighteen months, our second child, a girl, arrived. It was with the third pregnancy and the birth of Mark that the trouble began. Septicemia nearly cost Julie her life and the four operations which followed left her in a state of total exhaustion. Her courage and her will to live made me blind to her terrible suffering. I continued to get further involved at work and in my political activities. The second great love of my life was skiing, which I thoughtlessly indulged in on my days off. Since Julie did not seem to mind, I just took off on my own, never hesitating for a moment.

Julie: After undergoing all these operations I felt as if my body was beginning to crack and I grew ever more fragile. At this stage, my childhood and all the suffering I had known came to the surface again. I no longer had any illusions about my relationship with Billy. Things I might have put up with when I was physically strong, just got to be too much for me. I felt betrayed and could not rely on Billy's presence or help as he was so busy with his own life. Little by little, the cracks were beginning to affect my mind. Everything pointed to the inevitable breakdown of our family. I no longer cared whether Billy was with me or not. On the contrary, the house, the family, and the children, were like a prison. I tried to get out of the house as much as possible, not caring about anything else. I thought I ought to go out and enjoy myself, to make friends and to meet other people. But truthfully, I soon realized that such an escape route would have become an even more confining prison than the one I was trying to get away from. The only thing left was to escape from life itself — and I tried to do just that.

Billy: It was in this dramatic setting that I saw my castle fall to pieces and with it my self-esteem. My wife was in the hospital and I was at home with three small children and no idea how to look after them.

I was desperate, and saw no solution in sight. A few months earlier I had met a doctor who had left a great impression on me. He believed in people and in his work. I decided to go to him and ask his advice on how to behave towards Julie once she was out of danger and able to come home. His answer struck me as both odd and quite out of keeping with his profession. "Look," he told me, "when your wife is back with you, try to love her, just as she is, without reproaching her. Try to do whatever she asks, if it is at all possible. If she doesn't feel like talking, don't you talk either. If on the other hand she does, then talk with her, and above all, listen." It seemed an absurd prescription, rather simplistic. I was all ready to reject it, but he said to me, "Try it, just for a month. Let's give it a chance, then we'll see." "Well, a month isn't very long," I said to myself.

During those first few days I thought I was going mad. This remedy was so far removed from my normal routine that I felt crushed, completely overwhelmed by the effort. I was so used to doing things as I pleased, that this attempt to please someone else was taking its toll on me both physically and mentally. Still, I tried to keep going. "Just one month," I kept telling myself. During this experimental phase, while Julie rested, I used to sit down and read. I always had a passion for reading. Then one day I came across a book I didn't know we had in the house—the Bible.

I started to pick it up from time to time, and read it as though I were accepting a challenge, ready to throw it into a corner as soon as it began to annoy me. However, the more it annoyed me (since it made me recognize my way of life), the more I felt compelled to read it, and to continue all the way to the end. I couldn't explain why I felt there was a certain similarity between the words I read and the advice the doctor gave me. Reading the Bible also made me recall a priest who had been in charge of a parish in my town for several years. I had spoken to him briefly on various occasions, but had not managed to pin a label on him — which was what I usually did to people. Other people whom I had recently met also came to mind and I found a correlation between them and what Jesus says about those who want to follow him. I was now seeing my own experience with Julie in light of all that I read. Above all, I had the distinct feeling that it was not ideas or facts that I had come up against, but a person. The old Billy objected to what seemed like giving in to sentiment, but there was no way out of it. The truth is that I felt very strongly that I was in the company of a real friend, and from this relationship I drew the strength to go forward.

Time passed very quickly and I found myself at the end of the month's treatment. I went back to the doctor, not to tell him, as I had thought I would, how ridiculous the treatment was, but to tell about its effects (on me as well) and that I wanted to continue with it. Until then I had enjoyed myself in lots of ways and been interested in all sorts of things. I had been happy, but never quite experienced what I was experiencing now. When I managed to contain my impatience and irritation at one of Julie's outbursts, or through one of her long monologues, I experienced something completely new within me, a subtle joy, gentle and comforting, far removed from euphoria and exultation. A profound inner peace filled me. Further still, Julie herself seemed unexpectedly different. I discovered the treasures hidden within her — her limpid personality, her purity, her generosity. I was beginning to get to know her and beginning to love her.

Julie: When I came out of the hospital, I realized how difficult it was going to be to resume my place in the home. I could see that Billy was different somehow. In fact, little by little, I noticed him changing, but I didn't stop to think about it, because I just wasn't interested in what lay behind it. I no longer believed in any of the pretenses which Billy had assumed during our life together. "You have made me suffer so much with your indifference," I thought, "and now you think you can get around me with a few soft words."

I set myself a goal: I was going to unmask him. Naturally I used the weapons I had. I tried to nail him with harsh words and stinging phrases. Sometimes, at the beginning, he would lose control and react, but most of the time he accepted and continued on. I was really becoming cruel, and yet, my own attitude was leaving me ill at ease. The more I provoked and wounded him, the more at peace he seemed. "Has he really changed, after all?" I asked myself. How had he managed it alone? He had started to visit the doctor, then his family and others as well. Later, when he introduced them to me, the picture became clearer. I saw in those people an attitude similar to the one that had so astonished me in Billy. I learned from them that they were involved in trying to build relationships on a new basis, on a love that was quite different from the kind I had known. In the beginning, I gave them a hard time, as I did to Billy, but eventually I had to give in. I started to feel the guilt. My weapons were destroyed, and really, it became easy then. I looked beyond myself, first at Billy, then at the children, and finally at everybody else.

It's strange—because of Billy I almost threw my life away, and because of Billy, I have found a new life. Now, whenever we are with the children in the evening or on Sundays, and I see what a wonderful father Billy is, or when we are all together in the mountains and he is teaching them to ski, when he shows affection to me or says something funny, I feel that everything is getting back to normal. I feel certain that the time will come when all bitterness will disappear, without leaving any trace behind.

J. and B. C.

BEHIND THE EVENTS

My husband is the soccer coach of my five-year-old boy's team. One October day it became dark before practice ended. I was loading some of the equipment into the trunk of the car while my husband was talking with some of the parents. Suddenly my little boy darted out into the middle of the street. I saw a car coming and it hit him head on. It threw him quite a distance.

My reaction was one of desperation. I screamed and went running to him. He lay in the street in the fetal position staring into space with no movement or response to my voice. I felt completely helpless. I wanted to do something but I was afraid to move him. I just stood there screaming and I could hear people around me yelling for someone to call an ambulance.

All of a sudden I remembered Mary standing desolate at the foot of the cross, standing before her dying son. I then knew God was asking me to make this a sacred moment. I knew the most valuable thing I could do for my little boy was to be silent as Mary was, to be ready for anything, and to face it with love. A great peace and strength came over me as I said my yes to this unexpected misfortune. I understood that to love God with my whole heart I must be willing to give him back my child if that was what he was asking of me.

My husband's immediate reaction was not to wait for the medical team but to pick him up and rush to the emergency room ourselves. On the way to the hospital we prayed together again. My husband and I belong to different Churches and I had never experienced such unity with him, unity that only suffering could bring. When we were almost at the hospital, our little boy started to cry. What an answer to our prayers. It was only then that we knew for sure that he was alive. When we arrived at the emergency room, the doctors asked that only one parent accompany the child in. When I saw the look in my husband's eyes, I knew I should be the one to stay behind. It was another moment to die to myself and be free of everything, a moment to totally trust in God's love. Shortly after, however, they called for me to come, too. At first my son was unaware of our presence. Each time the doctors came into the room, they would tell us of another X-ray they were going to take, but they would not say anything about his condition. It was not until midnight that we finally were told the test results. One of the doctors commented to us that it was a miracle that he had survived, and had not suffered head injuries. As he walked out, he told us we should give a course to other parents on how to stay calm in times of crises.

When the police arrived at the hospital to get a statement from us I asked if the woman who drove the car knew that our boy was alive. The officer believed she did not so I asked him if he could return to her to let her know.

The next morning she came to the hospital. You can imagine her pain. She thanked me for asking the policeman to notify her and informed me that she had not left the scene of the accident. She had remained there nearly hysterical thinking that she had killed our son. When she approached his bedside, he smiled at her and said hello. It made me think about what Jesus had said that if we don't become like children we cannot enter the kingdom of heaven (cf. Mk 10:15).

The next day the doctors came in to tell us what we were facing. My son had a major fracture of the femur bone. He would either stay in the hospital for three months in traction or be sent home in a body cast for four or five months. It would take a couple of days to determine which was best for him. The doctors said that it was a delicate break in a child this age because of the rapid growth and that there was a possibility he might limp for the rest of his life. Each moment of those first days was filled with the unknown. The temptation was strong to slip into worrying about the future but I knew I had to live well each moment, rooted in love.

After the third day we were told that the decision was made in favor of the body cast. It was hard to imagine this five-year-old in a body cast. Many things in my life had to be changed in order to live out this new will of God. One of them was to immediately quit my job. Working had become necessary for the last two years because my husband's industry was undergoing a slowdown.

When I went in to request personal leave without pay, the management gave me an advance on my spring vacation pay and an extra month's salary. My husband was able to change jobs, obtain a higher salary, and work out of our home. This meant that he was also more available to lift our son when necessary. All of these occurrences were part of a beautiful plan of God that I could never have worked out. We did fine at home; my son took the body cast very well and never complained. He had to be waited on like an infant but it made me very happy because it gave me an opportunity day by day to unite myself to Jesus through this suffering.

Every time we went to the doctors to get X-rays taken, they told us how important it was to keep the cast on until the bone healed. However, on New Year's Day, my son came down with a terrible case of chicken pox. After three days he was so uncomfortable that the doctor made the decision to remove the cast in order to avoid infection. This implied a big step for me. I was afraid we were removing the cast too soon. Then I realized that God allows everything to happen for a reason and I needed to have full trust in him. I was really struggling with wanting to know who it might have been that came to our house with the chicken pox without saying so. I struggled with my anger over the inconvenience it was causing. Then I remember picking up a meditation written by Chiara Lubich. "If we look at suffering," I read, "only from the human point of view we will be tempted to look for the cause and not go one step further. We forget that behind the events of our lives there is God with his love who wills or permits everything that happens to us for a higher reason, for our good."

I was so happy to read this. I wanted to take everything as coming from the hands of God; it didn't matter to me anymore where the chicken pox came from.

My son is walking now and has very little visible effects from the accident. What *is* visible and lasting is the unity that these five months have built among my family and friends.

R.M.

PART OF THE "ONE FAMILY"

Charles: Mary and I are from central Indiana. We have four children. This particular experience of ours began at a time when Mary was in the hospital. It was not an easy time for us because we had just lost a baby. At that same time, I also had heard that the father of a family of twelve children in our neighborhood was in the hospital due to an accident. Realizing that his wife was in a similar circumstance as my own, I decided to find out if she needed some kind of assistance. With a couple of our children I went over to her home and introduced myself. She told me that everything was going O.K. and that some of the other neighbors had been of great help.

While I was in the house, I could not help but notice it was in very bad shape, structurally. The father had just finished renovating the dining room before his accident. The rest of the house had plaster falling down, and many other problems.

The next day I met with a particular group of families that I see every so often. The reason we are in frequent contact with one another is to share our desire and efforts in putting the gospel message into practice. I took the chance to let them know about the family I visited and about the condition of their house. They took interest in it themselves, and we decided to see if we could help out in some way to complete the renovation while the father was recuperating in the hospital.

In trying to present our idea in a way most understandable to the mother of the family, I suggested that some of us, together with herself and her children, could finish the rest of the house as a surprise for her husband. She agreed.

Love is very contagious. The small group that began working on the house evenings and weekends grew every day. For example, a soap distributor came to deliver cleaning material. Once he realized what was happening, he and his wife began working with us. We needed a good bit of plasterboard, floor covering, paint, and so on. The materials seemed to appear providentially, mostly in the form of non-saleable items that local merchants "just happened to have lying around."

The most beautiful thing about this project was the atmosphere among those working on the house. The workers were generous in contributing as well as giving up their own ideas. When the house was finished, it looked great. To see the change was a joy in itself, but the greatest joy was the atmosphere of mutual love among us.

A few days later, one of the couples knocked on our door. We sat down together, and they asked if I could help them understand the special atmosphere that existed among those of us working on the house. They said that it seemed almost like a "presence."

I was able to explain to them the words of Jesus, "Where two or more are gathered in my name, there am I in the midst of them" (Mt 18:20). We also remembered the disciples at Emmaus saying in the gospel account, "Were not our hearts burning inside us as he talked to us on the road and explained the scriptures to us" (Lk 24:32). The couple understood, and to this day they try with the rest of us to keep Jesus alive in our midst through mutual love.

Mary: There were many benefits also for those who started out as the "benefactors" in our adventure. We all became recipients of the fruits of mutual love. One family, who no longer had small children of their own, took the three youngest children on several occasions, allowing the mother to be with her husband in the hospital. The mutual love within that large family, as witnessed by the love among the small children, was an inspiration to those who took them in, and through them, to the other families involved. It was clear that despite the lack of many material items, this was a family truly rich in love.

Several years have passed and a close relationship remains between this family and our little group of families. Although the parents know of our strong commitment to living the gospel, they have not felt drawn, nor obligated to join us in this way. Instead, they have felt perfectly free to remain a part of our larger extended family. In this way, the bond among us continues to grow.

One evening we learned of a tragic occurrence. One of their daughters, a sophomore at the State University, had been killed in a car accident on her way home for the summer. Our first thought was to go to be with the family. Almost immediately, though, we wondered, "Are we really that close to them, that we would not be intruding?" But love prompted us to go. They welcomed us as members of the one family we had become, and we saw that it was the right decision to make. It was a very profound experience to be together, sharing in their deep grief, but sharing also the memorable events of their daughter's short but full life.

Recently, friends of ours had brought groceries to be shared with others in need. Among the items we had received was a frozen turkey. We gave it to this family, explaining that it had been given to us and that we wanted them to have it. We had planned to take the rest of the groceries to the local Caring Center which provides aid for stricken families, but something made us hesitate. Shortly after, we learned that another family had given groceries to this family and that it had been very gratefully received. Something made us feel that they were in more need than we had originally thought. We decided that the rest of what we had received should also go to them. Later, we learned through one of the children that although their mother had not yet found a job, their father had. We understood that both parents had been unemployed at that time. We also realized that these children too, see us as members of the same family.

Charles: This whole experience, I believe, left a lasting mark on all of us, and certainly on our children. As our children grow older I can see a certain "family trait" to be open to others with actions as well as with sincere concern. It is also beautiful to see the extended family relationship that exists between all of the families enriched by this relationship of concrete mutual love.

C. & M. W.

BIRTH DEFECT

In April, our second baby, a boy, was born with a very serious birth defect. The spinal fluid had formed a sac attached to his head. There was no certainty that he would live and there was a need for immediate surgery to remove the sac.

For my husband and I, it was a shock especially when a doctor, an intern, told us mistakenly that there would be definite mental retardation. The most advanced test, in fact, showed that there was brain tissue in the fluid sac. The doctors waited four days before Sam's operation so that he would be stronger physically.

During these days, I realized more fully that to believe in God's love, and therefore to trust in him, meant that I had to reach out to those in the hospital around me. I could make myself one with the other mothers with their new babies by keeping them company, by helping them when the nurses were not available, forgetting about my own suffering which included the fact that Sam had been transferred to the intensive care unit of still another hospital.

I remember at times, crying when praying to God, asking for the grace to believe in his love, and I found peace. I think that the others felt that my love for them had a deeper source. One of the mothers still calls me and has even given me various baby items she no longer needed.

One of the nurses, who was deciding whether or not to get married, asked me for advice. I realized that she really needed someone who could listen to her. Before I left the hospital she asked for my address so that she could invite me to the wedding reception.

Finally, the four days had gone by and the doctor allowed me to go home as long as I did not go to the other hospital to visit Sam on account of his operation, which happened to be the very same day. Even though this was difficult for me, I recognized God's will in this too. My husband went to visit Sam and stayed with him for a while. The fact that he went alone, he said, had given him the chance to become more aware of his role as a father.

I remember that many of our friends were praying on the day of the operation and when the doctor began to operate, he found that the test results had been wrong. There was no brain tissue in the sac. Sam survived the operation and was sent home on Mother's Day.

He came home very weak and slept a great deal. Every time I looked at him, I had to constantly remember to embrace this suffering with love, because the doctor could not be sure how he would develop or if there was any brain damage. Trying to believe in love, little by little I found myself more capable of treating those around me with more understanding. When I told the others the experience of what had happened, they asked me how my husband and I could be so calm. On these occasions I shared how we draw our strength from our faith in the gospel. We were often understood.

In November we had to make another decision. We had known that Sam needed another operation to correct the shape of his head. It was very difficult to agree on the date for the operation. To our dismay, the hospital called us on Thanksgiving Day asking us to bring the baby in that afternoon. Apparently, the receptionist had forgotten to notify us beforehand. Again we took the step to place Sam in God's hands, trusting in his will.

The surgery was successful, but afterwards Sam looked so weak. What a sight to see the bandages wrapped like a turban around his head. As I went each day to visit him, I felt more aware how precious these moments were. I could learn to make use of all the suffering I was experiencing to help me love in a greater capacity. There were many chances to do so. For example, when the maternity nurses noticed that I had come, they would take the opportunity to ask me how Sam was doing and would want to spend some time with him. I allowed them to be with Sam, though I had longed to take care of him myself. The nurses couldn't get over how happy the baby was.

Again in February, there was another similar operation, and this time, because I had grown to love Sam even more, it was also harder to be ready to give him back to God. I kept the same attitude toward the nurses and it was like seeing old friends again. Sam recovered so well from the operation that one of the nurses remarked, "If Sam keeps being so good-natured, he will grow up to be a saint!"

This time it was the nurses who thought of me. Love was becoming mutual. There had been a mix-up about Sam's discharge and the doctor never came. The night nurse made a special call to the doctor and made arrangements, so when I was ready to go home, she said that I could take Sam with me. I was so happy! One of the nurses' aides was even crying a little when we left.

Those days in the hospital became a joy for me and a rapport was built with the staff which I think will remain. This experience helped me to realize even more how God loves each one of us personally, and that when we love, especially when it is difficult, the love which we receive in return is something which fills us completely, as a gift that comes directly from God.

P. T.

* * *

The experiences of this section witness to a natural tendency of the Christian community, of the family united with one another, to reach out in service to others. *Isn't this the litmus test of teaching in the way that Jesus did? He taught in stories of service to others and he witnessed over and over again to actions of loving service to others.*

Brian and Lorraine remind us of the environment in which the family must live, one of consumerism and indulgence, in which the models of family living presented, so often are centered on material things rather than the call to be sister and brother to our neighbors.

Out of an environment of giving and sharing, of forgiving, of being united with the pain or joy of the other person, comes the response to the call to service. "The Gift of Faith" shares the experience of living in this way in relation to the needs of another family. The will to serve intensifies the bond of unity with others. It calls us to unite with the sufferings and cross of others as our own. Julie's experience shows us how this unity grows and matures inviting us to see others with new eyes each time we meet them.

The experiences of several families in this section remind us of the gospel reports of events in the life of Mary, the Mother of Jesus. Her visit to Elizabeth, her hospitality, her love can be seen in the experience of Charles and Mary, who see in service to others, the contagious quality of love. They build in this way an "extended family," enriched by the relationship of mutual love. At the same time they see service to others, "actions as well as sincere concern" becoming a "family trait" in their children.

Love seeks expression in serving. It builds unity. When it becomes mutual love, we have the assurance of the presence of Jesus. The political and social problems and issues of our times as well as the problems of family life, find solutions in this environment of constant and mutual love.

111